THE MOUNTAIN BIKE GUIDE TO

THE BRECON BEACONS
NATIONAL PARK & THE
BLACK MOUNTAINS

20 ALL TERRAIN RIDES COMPILED
AND PHOTOGRAPHED BY NICK COTTON

ISBN 871890 24 1

PUBLISHED BY CORDEE

CONTENTS

The Brecon Beacons, which also include the Black Mountains, offer the enthusiast some of the finest mountain biking in southern Britain. The limestone and red sandstone hills, rising to almost 3000 feet, are criss-crossed by hundreds of miles of byways, bridleways, unclassified roads, dismantled railway paths and forestry tracks offering something for everyone from the novice to the downhill headbanger. The underlying rock means that the tracks are rideable for far more of the year than those lying on the chalk and Oolithic Limestone south and east of Britain's geological divide – an imaginary line drawn from Exeter to Scarborough. With its links to the motorway network, South Wales lies within three hours of over half the population of Britain: London, Birmingham, Manchester and most of the population between can easily access the rugged grandeur of the Brecons Beacons National Park.

The area covered by this book divides naturally into three main areas:
In the west three rides start from or near Sennybridge; there are five in the central area, the Brecon Beacons proper, and a further nine in the Black Mountains to the northeast. The remaining three rides are at the southwest, southeast and northern fringes.

BRECON BEACONS NATIONAL PARK

The Brecon Beacons National Park consists of three separate ranges of hills and their names (together with the name of the National Park itself) often cause confusion. To the east are The Black Mountains (with an 's' !), the toughest ride in the book (Grwyne Fawr) and the steepest climbs lie within this area, notably the lung-bursting ascents of the scarp face on Lord Hereford's Knob (Ride 19), Y Dâs (Ride 15), the rough crossing from the Honddu to Grwyne Fawr valleys near to Llanthony (Ride 17) and the shorter but equally fierce ascent of Mynydd Llangorse (Ride 13). This area is less busy than the Brecon Beacons, perhaps because it lacks the draw of the highest mountain in South Wales; it is certainly not for its lack of outstandingly beautiful moorland scenery.

In the centre are The Brecon Beacons which rise to 2908 ft (886 mts) on Pen y Fan, including the classic mountain bike pass through the range between Cribyn and Fan y Big (10 miles north of Merthyr Tydfil, above the Upper Neuadd Reservoir). This pass, at almost 2000 feet, is ridden in each direction in Rides 6 and 7. The old Roman Road of Sarn Helen, connecting Neath to Brecon runs right across the area and is explored in Ride 5. Talybont-on-Usk, 6 miles southeast of Brecon is one of the best bases in the area: three rides in the book start from here, another four rides lie within 5 miles and the Taff Trail passes through on its way from Cardiff to Brecon. It is a small, attractive village with good pubs, a cafe and a village store.

To the west lies The Black Mountain, which is in fact not one summit but a collection of limestone hills rising to a highpoint of

2630 ft (802 mts) on Fan Brycheiniog. This area is disappointing from a mountain biking point of view: take a look at the map and your heart leaps at the sight of bridleways criss-crossing the range but these bridleways are by and large unrideable and in many cases non-existent on the ground. Stick to the lanes between the Black Mountain and Llandovery if you want to explore this area by bike.

MAPS

All the rides are contained on two Ordnance Survey Landranger 1:50,000 maps:

160 Brecon Beacons
161 Abergavenny and the Black Mountains

Alternatively you may prefer to use the larger scale Outdoor Leisure Maps (1:25,000) in which case the following will cover the rides in the Brecon Beacons and Black Mountains:

Outdoor Leisure 12
Brecon Beacons West and Central
Outdoor Leisure 13
Brecon Beacons East

ACCOMMODATION

The best way to find appropriate accommodation whether you are looking for a campsite or a five star hotel is to ring the Tourist Information Centre close to where you wish to stay.
If you call in at the TIC in person they will book the accommodation for you.
The numbers of the relevant Tourist Information Centres are shown below.
The best bases where you will find a variety of good accommodation, pubs, cafes and teashops tend to lie along the Usk Valley between Abergavenny and Brecon.
Places such as Crickhowell, Llangynidr, Talybont-on-Usk and Llanfrynach all have a variety of accommodation and good pubs.

To the north (for the Black Mountains) the Castle Inn at Pengenffordd (3 miles south of Talgarth on the A479) is highly recommended and it also has a Trekkers Barn Tel: 01874 711353.
Lying just to the north of the Black Mountains, Hay-on-Wye is one of the most interesting small towns in Britain. It is the centre of the second-hand book trade with loads of bookshops and cafes and makes a fine bolt hole should rain stop play and you need to kill a couple of hours while waiting for the weather to improve.

TOURIST INFORMATION CENTRES

Abergaveny Tel: 01873 857588
Brecon Tel: 01874 622485
Crickhowell Tel: 01873 812105
Hay on Wye Tel: 01497 820144
Merthyr Tydfil Tel: 01685 379884
Pontneddfechan Tel: 01639 721795

I have tried to include as wide a selection of rides in the main part of the book as possible. In this section, Other Routes in Brief, a few more ideas are suggested that need to be studied in conjunction with the appropriate Ordnance Survey map.

FORESTRY

Several rides described in the main section use Forestry Commission tracks. It is notoriously difficult to give directions in forests: there are few signposts, if any; no buildings, pubs or farms to use as bearings; no guarantee that what you see one year will still be there the next and a vocabulary limited to right, left, up, down and the number of tracks that you pass on your way.

However, in compensation, you do tend to get a reliable consistency and mixture of forest roads and single track in forestry holdings and if you enjoy the challenge of devising your own routes in areas where there is an open access policy, listed below are the forests in the region.

1. Llaneglwys Wood and Ysgywydd Hwch, between the B4520 and the A470, 6 miles north of Brecon. Partly explored in Ride 4, Mynydd Fforest and Llaneglwys Wood.

2. Mynydd Myddfai, Mynydd Wysg and Glasfynydd Forest around Usk Reservoir, south of the A40 between Sennybridge and Llandovery. This is partly explored in Ride 1, Usk Reservoir.

3. Coed y Rhaiadr and other nearby smaller holdings. North of Pontneddfechan, on the A465 halfway between Neath and Merthyr Tydfil. Partly explored in Ride 5, Pontneddfechan, Ystradfellte and Sarn Helen.

4. Coed Taf Fawr and Onllwyn near to Garwnant Visitor Centre, off the A470 to the north of Merthyr Tydfil. Partly explored in Ride 6, Six Reservoirs Challenge.

5. Talybont Forest, Tal Fechan Forest and other holdings around the reservoirs to the southwest of Talybont on Usk. Partly explored in Rides 6, 7, 8 and 9.

6. Mynydd Du Forest, northwest of Abergavenny. Partly explored in Rides 16, 17 and 18.

LANE NETWORKS

There may be times in the middle of winter when you want to go for a ride and cannot face the prospect of slow muddy tracks and would prefer to go for a blast on quiet lanes, knowing that you can cover a good distance without worrying about the surface you are riding on, without gates to open and happy that you can go into a pub in a reasonably presentable state. There are two areas which immediately spring to mind:

1. Around Brecon. To the west, north and east there are fine networks of lanes through beautiful scenery connecting Brecon to Llandovery, Llanwrtyd Wells, Builth Wells and Hay-on-Wye.
(**OS Landranger maps** *147, 148, 160, 161).*

2. The triangle formed by Hay-on-Wye, Newport and Ross-on-Wye is singularly ill-served by bridleways and offroad tracks. As compensation there are hundreds of miles

of excellent, quiet lanes linking many
attractive villages and the handsome towns of
Monmouth and Usk
(**OS Landranger maps** 161, 162, 171).

TO THE SOUTH

The area is covered by another book in this
series: **Mountain Bike Guide to the Valleys
of South Wales the Gower Peninsula and
Lower Wye Valley** (published by Cordee)
which describes 21 all terrain rides from the
white sand beaches of the Gower in the west
to the steep wooded hills of the Wye Valley in
the east together with many of the ridges
between old mining valleys of South Wales.

TO THE WEST

(Pembrokeshire and the coast).
 Draw a line north from Aberystwyth to
Swansea and you cut off the whole of the
'prong' of West Wales. Within this area there
are remarkably few offroad options: with the
exception of Brechfa Forest, to the northeast
of Camarthen and a few tracks over the
Preseli Hills, the area is almost devoid of good
offroad tracks. The lane network, however,
is excellent and the coastal walking around
the Pembrokeshire peninsula is some of the
best in Britain.

TO THE NORTH

By contrast with the area lying to the west,
Mid Wales has an abundance of excellent
mountain biking, including tracks around the
reservoirs of Llyn Briane and Claerwen,
the vast forestry holdings north of Llanwrtyd
Wells and to the east of Aberystwyth, and last
but far from least, the astonishing network
of byways and bridleways throughout Powys
and into Shropshire.

Good bases are New Radnor, Llanwrtyd Wells,
Rhayader, Llangurig, Knighton, Church
Stretton, Devil's Bridge and Machynlleth.

TO THE EAST

With the exceptions of the Monmouth-
Chepstow section of the Wye Valley and the
Forest of Dean there is little mountain biking
between the Rivers Usk and Severn. A large
part of this area falls within Herefordshire and
Worcestershire and one would be hard pushed
to find two counties with so little to offer for
the mountain biker. The theory is that a cabal
 of landowners ensured that following the
1947 Wildlife and Countryside Act, when
rights of way were being put on to definitive
maps, any 'claimed' paths that were accepted
into the new network were given the lowest
status, ie footpath rather than bridleway or
byway.

AROUND THE USK RESERVOIR WEST OF TRECASTLE

DISTANCE
17 miles (27 kms)

TIME
3 hours

GRADE
Moderate

TERRAIN
Moorland, forestry, reservoir

HILLS AND HIGHPOINTS
1st climb ▲ 585 ft (178 mts)
from Trecastle onto the moorlands
2nd climb ▲ 230 ft (70 mts)
from Usk Reservoir to south of the forestry
Highest point ▲ 1340 ft (408 mts)
near to the old Roman Camp
Total ascent ▲ 985 ft (300 mts)

START
The large layby on the A40 at the
western end of Trecastle
(between Brecon and Llandovery)

PARKING
The large layby on the A40

NEAREST RAILWAY
Llandovery, 5 miles northwest of the route
near the Roman Camp at Instruction 2

REFRESHMENTS
Castle Coaching Inn, Three Horseshoes
PH, Trecastle

There are several Roman forts in the area and soon after leaving Trecastle you find yourself climbing steeply on a Roman road to what must have been one of their bleaker outposts at Y Pigwyn. Here the route swings south off the moorland to enter the forestry that encircles the reservoir.

This is the most westerly of the rides featured in the book: further north there are plenty of tracks through Crychan Forest and around Llyne Briane Reservoir; to the west, right as far as the Pembrokeshire Coast, there is little offroad riding at all with the exception of Brechfa Forest and one track across the Preseli Hills; to the northeast is danger territory in the form of the artillery and rifle ranges on Mynydd Eppynt; and to the south the Black Mountain is a huge disappointment – crossed in several places by bridleways, these are often no more than lines drawn on the map with no corresponding track on the ground. So... make the most of the Usk Reservoir and the tracks through the forestry which surround it! After a short section back on the moorland around the head of a dry valley, the network of quiet lanes is joined for a long descent back to Trecastle.

1 With your back to the Post Office in Trecastle **turn L** then take the **1st road L** climbing steeply away from the A40. After $1/2$ mile take the **1st lane to the R** (no signpost). Continue climbing as the gradient eases.

2 The tarmac lane turns to a good quality stone track. Fine views down into the Usk Reservoir. Go past 1st wooden signpost with 'Please control your dog'. **Easily missed**, shortly after the grassy hummocks of the Roman Camp to the right and left and just by a 2nd wooden post with the same dog warning **bear L** onto grassy track heading towards the top of the nearest large hill.

3 **Take the right hand fork at two junctions**, continuing towards the summit. At a junction of several tracks at the bottom of a small dip **turn L** downhill towards forestry plantation and the sharp profile of Bannau Sir Gaer, Fan Foel and Fan Brycheiniog.

4 Follow the stone-based then grassy track to the green gate into the forest. **Ignore** the left turn in a large gravel clearing. Continue downhill. At T-junction with the road **turn R** then after 200 yards, opposite the parking area **bear R** uphill onto broad forestry track and shortly **fork L**.

5 Follow the track around the edge of the reservoir. Cross one river via bridge and second river via stepping stones. Cross the road and go **SA** onto forestry track.

6 Climb for 1 mile. Immediately after two tracks join from the left take the **next R** through gate to exit forestry. **Ignore** the main track ahead towards stone sheds. Instead, **bear L** and soon pick up a well-defined track parallel to and 100 yards from the edge of the forestry to the left.

7 At the junction of tracks at the head of a dry valley **turn L** and aim for the gate in the wall/fence. One short boggy section. The track soon improves and becomes an enclosed track. Go past farm and cross stream to join tarmac lane. At the second farm **turn sharp L**.

8 After 2 miles, at T-junction **turn R** to cross bridge. After further 2 miles, at T-junction with the A40 in Trecastle **turn L** to return to the start.

THE OLD COACH ROAD OVER BRYN MELYN, SOUTH OF SENNYBRIDGE

DISTANCE
20 miles (32 kms)

TIME
4 hours

GRADE
Strenuous

TERRAIN
Pasture and broadleaf woodland, moorland.
Scattered stone farmhouses

HILLS AND HIGHPOINTS
Four main climbs, three in the first half of
the ride, one in the second half:
1st climb ▲ 330 ft (100 mts)
steep road climb at the start
2nd climb ▲ 425 ft (130 mts)
steep track starting the offroad section
3rd climb ▲ 490 ft (150 mts)
steady offroad climb up to Bryn Melyn
4th climb ▲ 490 ft (150 mts)
final steep road climb out of the Senni Valley
Highest point ▲ 1550 ft (473 mts)
on Bryn Melyn
Total ascent ▲ 2700 ft (825 mts)

START
Defynnog, a village 1 mile south of
Sennybridge on the A4067 towards Swansea

PARKING
Parking spaces near the telephone box,
by the church or 1st left off the A4215
towards the Post Office / stores

NEAREST RAILWAY
Llandovery, 13 miles to the west or Aberdare,
13 miles to the south

REFRESHMENTS
Tanners Arms PH, Defynnog

*I had the unusual experience
of cycling this section in a
blizzard in May with the snow
falling hard enough to settle
on my legs as I rode along.
White snow, white May
blossom, white cow parsley and
some very bemused-looking
swallows perched on a
telephone line!*

It is in Sennybridge that the River Usk, which eventually reaches the sea at Newport, becomes a river of real size. After leaving Usk Reservoir it is soon joined by the Rivers Crai, Cilieni and the Senni (from which Sennybridge derives its name). By the time the Usk reaches Brecon, swelled by water running off Mynydd Eppynt to the north and the Brecon Beacons to the south, the valley has widened with a much broader floodplain. This ride starts from the small village of Defynnog, a mile south of Sennybridge, soon climbing to close to 1000 feet. Shortly after leaving tarmac at the farm of Camlais Uchaf you are faced with a steep but beautiful push up through broadleaf woodland to join the course of what looks like an old coach road across the plateau. The A4215 is crossed and you are soon onto the wide, stone-based track that climbs to over 1500 ft on Bryn Melyn with fine views down into the Senni Valley. The road is followed down hairpin bends into the valley before climbing once again for an offroad ridge ride almost all the way back to Defynnog.

This ride could easily be linked to the Pontneddfechan / Ystradfellte ride (Ride 5) for a tough 40 mile challenge.

1 *From Defynnog take the A4215 signposted 'Merthyr Tydfil (A470)' then after 400 yards, soon after passing pottery/gallery on the right,* **turn L** *onto narrow lane between houses, one of which is called 'Penpentre'.*

2 *Steep climb then short descent. At T-junction with farmhouse ahead* **turn R then immediately R** *again steeply uphill on minor lane.*

3 **Ignore** *two right turns on tarmac lanes. On sharp left hand bend shortly after the second of these two lanes* **bear R** *through the concrete farmyard of Camlais Uchaf passing between the stone barns (signposted 'Bridleway').*

4 *Descend to the river, follow it briefly then cross it via ford or footbridge.* **Do not follow the main track as it swings left to** *cross a second river but* **bear R** *uphill away from this to join a sunken track via a metal gate with blue arrow waymark.*

5 *Climb steeply through 2nd metal gate. At the 3rd metal gate* **bear L** *away from the fence to continue steeply uphill on sunken track. This section may be muddy. Keep following the blue arrows through several more gates (wooden bridlegates, wood and metal field gates). The track broadens and levels out.*

6 *At X-roads with tarmac lane near to a pond go* **SA** *onto obvious track* **(not the track right next to the pond)**. *There are several tracks over the open pastureland. You are aiming towards the highpoint on the horizon (Pen y Fan/Corn Du), just to the left of the farm buildings. At T-junction with fence/line of trees* **turn R** *towards farm buildings.*

7 *At X-roads with road go* **SA** *'Forest Lodge 1'. After 3/4 mile, as the tarmac swings right,* **bear L** *(in effect SA) through gate onto track.*

8 *Follow this wonderful, well-made track for 6 miles, climbing to the highpoint of the ride at 1550 ft (473 mts). Two steep stony climbs, each follows a crossing of a side stream.*

9 *At T-junction with road turn* **sharp R*** *and climb steadily for 1 mile.*

* (For link to Ride 5 (Pontneddfechan-Ystradfellte) **turn L here** *then after 1 1/2 miles* **turn R** *through gate onto forestry track and join the other ride at the second part of Instruction 6).*

10 *After 1 mile of hairpin descents, at the bottom of the hill, shortly after crossing cattle grid, take the* **1st lane to the L**.

11 *At T-junction* after 2 more undulating miles, with a bridge to the right,* **turn L** *'Crai 4 1/2, Ystradgynlais 13 1/2'.*

* (Short cut. At the T-junction **turn R**, *cross bridge then after 1/2 mile* **1st lane to the L**. *At T-junction with A4215* **turn L** *to return to the start).*

12 *Steep climb on road. After 1 mile, and 100 yards after the end of the woodland on the right,* **turn R** *through gate onto track 'Bridleway'.*

13 *Go* **SA** *at X-roads of tracks and follow the bridleway round to the right by laid hedge. The track improves and turns to tarmac.*

14 **Easily missed***, 400 yards after passing cemetery on the right, on a sharp right hand bend* **bear L** *into field via gate signposted 'Public Footpath' (there is also a bridleway running parallel).*

15 *Follow the well-waymarked track through several recently replaced gates, climbing then descending. Some rough grassy sections where you may have to push.*

16 *Go down through final field. At T-junction with lane* **turn L***. At T-junction with main road (A4067)* **turn R** *to return to the start.*

TWO RIDGES NORTH OF SENNYBRIDGE

DISTANCE
20 miles (32 kms)

TIME
4 hours

GRADE
Strenuous

TERRAIN
Quiet lanes, river valley, pasture and moorland

HILLS AND HIGHPOINTS
1st climb ▲ 595 ft (182 mts)
from Pentre'r felin to the brow of the hill
2nd climb ▲ 320 ft (97 mts)
to the highpoint on the first moorland ridge
3nd climb ▲ 625 ft (190 mts)
from Aberbran to the next moorland top
4th climb ▲ 280 ft (86 mts)
from the lane at Instruction 10 to the
standing stone of Maen Richard
5th climb ▲ 510 ft (155 mts)
southeast from Llanfihangel Nant Bran
Highest point ▲ 1385 ft (422 mts)
at the standing stone of Maen Richard
Total ascent ▲ 2750 ft (840 mts)

START
The Post Office, Sennybridge, on the A40
between Brecon and Llandovery

PARKING
In the free car park opposite the Post Office
in Sennybridge

NEAREST RAILWAY
Llandovery, 12 miles to the west

REFRESHMENTS
Cafe, pubs, stores in Sennybridge

To the north of Sennybridge lies the army training area of Mynnydd Eppynt with regular artillery training creating a barrage of noise. Unsurprisingly, mountain biking on the bridleways through the danger areas is not recommended. This ride stays to the south of the shells and bullets.

The ride links two ridges either side of the Nant Bran River flowing down from Mynydd Eppynt to join the River Usk near to Aberbran. A steep road climb up from Pentre'r Felin takes you up to the first (undulating) ridge, passing two ponds with odd cairns built in the centre of them. A fast descent to Trallong is followed by the climb up onto the second ridge and the standing stone of Maen Richard. The descent down the valley of Cwm Erchan is ever more wooded to the hamlet of Llanfihangel Nant Bran. A steep road climb links you to the outward route back to Sennybridge.

1 With your back to the Post Office in Sennybridge **turn L** on the A40 toward Brecon. After 400 yards take the **1st road L** signposted 'Pentre'r Felin 1'.

2 Follow this road through Pentre'r Felin, following signs for Llanfihangel Nant Bran. 1/2 mile after the village **bear R** at fork (Shoemakers PH signposted to the left) and climb, steadily then steeply.

3 At the brow of the hill, just after a broad stone track to the left and just before the cattle grid across the road **turn R** onto grassy track alongside the fence.

4 **Easily missed**, 50 yards before the start of the conifer plantation on the left **bear R** on rough grassy track between gorse bushes towards the right-hand fence. Climb to the brow of the hill. The way ahead is now obvious, a grassy descent then a climb up through bracken.

5 Go past two ponds with cairns in the middle. Descend then climb, twice. At a X-roads of grassy tracks at the bottom of the third short descent **bear R**.

6 Track turns to tarmac. At the T-junction with Trallong Post Office ahead **turn L*** and follow road for 1 1/2 miles passing through the hamlet of Aberbran.

* (For Short Cut turn R here and return to Sennybridge**).**

7 **Full route**. Cross a stone bridge over the river then after 1/2 mile **turn L** onto road by triangle of grass signposted 'Llanfihangel Nant Bran 4 1/2'. Immediately after the barn on the right (with 'Llwyn y Merched' plaque) **turn R** onto track.

8 At the end of the stone track **turn L** uphill through field following tractor tracks. This becomes a muddy sunken lane for 200 yards. At a stone barn **turn R** through gate and **diagonally R** through field. At next gate **turn L** uphill alongside fence, following to the next gate then continuing uphill around the edge of the field.

9 Exit field onto broad track with trees either side. Continue in same direction onto grassy moorland track, **bearing L** at the first fork alongside the wall. At a 5 way junction of tracks go **SA** onto the steeper (left hand) of the two tracks heading for the top of the hill. At the next fork **bear R** onto the lower, more defined track.

10 At T-junction with road **bear L** then after 1 mile take the **1st road R**. Climb for 1/2 mile then as the lane swings sharp right (GR 978340) **bear L** (in effect SA) over cattle grid. Climb steeply. At the brow of the hill **turn L** onto broad grassy track towards standing stone of Maen Richard and the trig point.

11 At the trig point **turn R** (north). This track soon becomes more defined and turns into a broad grassy descent. At a X-roads of grassy tracks immediately after crossing the stream bed **turn L**.

12 Long descent on ever improving track. At T-junction with tarmac **turn R**. At T-junction with the road through Llanfihangel Nant Bran **turn R** to go past church then shortly take the **1st road L** 'Sennybridge 4 1/2'.

13 Steep climb then fast descent. At T-junction on descent **bear L**. Cross the bridge and follow the road round to the left 'Sennybridge 1 1/4'. At T-junction with A40 **turn R** to return to the Post Office.

Ride 3 ◄

Ride 3 ◄

Ride 4 ◄

◄ *Ride 2*

Ride 2 ►

PENTRE'R FELIN 2¼

TRALLONG 1¼
CRADOC 4½

TO MAIN ROAD
A40 ½

MYNYDD FFOREST AND LLANEGLWYS WOOD, NORTH OF BRECON

DISTANCE
15 miles (24 kms)

TIME
3 hours

GRADE
Moderate

TERRAIN
Moorland, forestry, pasture, fine views.
The surface varies from faint grassy tracks
to forestry roads

HILLS AND HIGHPOINTS
1st climb ▲ 755 ft (230 mts)
from the crossing of Sgithwen Brook
to the moorland above Llaneglwys Wood
2nd climb ▲ 330 ft (100 mts)
in Llaneglwys Wood
3rd climb ▲ 295 ft (90 mts)
returning to Brechfa Pool
Highest point ▲ 1380 feet (420 mts)
in Llaneglwys Wood
Total ascent ▲ 2300 ft (700 mts)

START
Brechfa Pool (GR 118318) to the west of
Llyswen (near the junction of the A470 and
A479, 4 miles northwest of Talgarth).
The minor road off the A470 which leads to
Brechfa Pool is near the brow of the hill with
a sign for 'Windycote Bed and Breakfast'

PARKING
Anywhere on the common near to
Brechfa Pool / the telephone box

NEAREST RAILWAY
Builth Road, 12 miles north of the route

REFRESHMENTS
None en route. Pub and stores (at garage)
in Llyswen

*Situated above the upper
Wye valley, the ride starts from
Brechfa Pool, a small but
extraordinary and atmospheric
lake, covered in wildfowl, with
the Black Mountains forming
an impressive backdrop to the
southeast. There is a real
'back of beyond' feel to
the area.*

This is the northernmost of the rides included in this book. The ride links together grass and stone bridleways with tiny farm lanes, passing through a mixture of broadleaf and coniferous woodland, sheep pasture and open moorland, rising to over 1300 feet. The ride described is just one of many that could be devised using the plethora of tracks and lanes that criss-cross the area between the River Wye in the east and the B4520 in the west. This is one of those rides where you need to prepare yourself in advance to end the ride with a climb rather than a descent.

1 *With back to the telephone box door* **turn L** *on road then* **fork L (not the** *'No through road').* After ¹/₂ mile take the **1st road to the L** 'Wernished Farm' then shortly, on left hand bend **bear R** onto grassy track towards the woodland.

2 *Join the grassy track running alongside the woodland and follow this for 1¹/₂ miles (at times wet with several small stream crossings).*

3 *At T-junction with the road* **turn R** *then, on a fast descent,* **1st road sharply L**. *Shortly* **bear L** *at a fork of lanes.*

4 *Follow through farm and several gates. Cross a stream, climb steeply, pass through a second farm. At T-junction with the road* **bear L**.

5 *After* ¹/₂ *mile, at the end of the woodland on the right* **turn R** *through gate onto track 'Tycanol'. At the house, go through gate and into yard then exit via gate in far right hand corner.* **Turn L** *steeply uphill along the left hand edge of the field.*

6 *At the top, go through two gates and* **turn L** *onto grassy track leading towards the summit. Superb views. Fine, well-drained grassy track. Descend to the road and* **bear L**.

7 *After* ¹/₂ *mile, at fork with a farm down to your left* **bear R** *uphill on broad stone track. At fork of tracks after* ¹/₂ *mile GR 062405)* **bear R**.

8 *At the end of well-defined path at a faint X-roads of grassy tracks on a wide grassy*

plateau go **SA** then shortly take the next **track to the L** to pass around the far side of the hill to your left.

9 *Enter the forestry and* **bear R** *uphill at fork of forestry roads.* **Ignore** *turnings to left and right. Descend then climb.*

10 *At the first major fork of tracks* ³/₄ *mile after the start of the climb* **bear R**. *There is a wooden marker post with 'C1' stamped on it (GR 045383).*

11 *Views open up to the right. Follow the main track as it starts descending. A track joins from the left (GR 044377).*

12 *Exit wood and continue on track in same direction. At T-junction with the road go* **SA** *through gate into field, following the right hand field edge. Through a second gate onto moorland, follow a grassy track parallel with the woodland to the left.*

13 *At T-junction with the next road* **turn R**. *Easily missed, after* ¹/₂ *mile, just before the brow of the hill* **turn L** *onto grassy track, soon* **forking R** *to pass to the right of hill summit.*

14 *Descend,* **bearing R** *to follow the fence / hedgerow. At T-junction with road* **turn R**, *then shortly take the 1st road to the L* 'No through road'. *After 50 yards* **bear R** *onto grassy track. The next section is hard to describe as there are many tracks: aim for the summit of the low hill ahead.*

15 *At the hill summit follow the main track to the east (towards the far end of the hills ahead). On descent* **bear L** *onto rough track. Join tarmac by cottage.*

16 *Descend through farm. At T-junction with road* **turn R** *then shortly at the next T-junction (by bridge)* **turn L**. *After 100 yards* **turn 1st R** *opposite house onto a broad stone track.*

17 *The gradient steepens. At road by farm* **bear L** *and follow this lane back to the start.*

PONTNEDDFECHAN, YSTRADFELLTE AND THE OLD ROMAN ROAD OF SARN HELEN

DISTANCE
Full route 22 miles (35 kms)
Short route 17 miles (28 kms)

TIME
Full route 4 hours
Short route 3 hours

GRADE
Strenuous

TERRAIN
Moorland, forestry, pasture, an old Roman road, old mining area around Dyffryn Cellwen

HILLS AND HIGHPOINTS
1st major climb ▲ 820 ft (250 mts) from the start to the top of Moel Penderyn
2nd major climb ▲ 560 ft (170 mts) from Ystradfellte to Plas-y-gors forestry
Highest point ▲ 1380 ft (420 mts) in Plas-y-gors forestry (Instruction 6)
Total ascent ▲ full route 2700 ft (820 mts)
▲ short route 2400 ft (730 mts)

START
The Craig y Ddinas car park at the eastern end of Pontneddfechan (just off the A465 halfway between Neath and Merthyr Tydfil). Take the lower road alongside the Craig y Ddinas Hotel. GR 911079

PARKING
The Craig y Ddinas car park

NEAREST RAILWAY
Neath, 11 miles southwest of Glyn Neath or Treherbert, 11 miles south of Penderyn

REFRESHMENTS
There are pubs and stores in Pontneddfechan, Penderyn and Glyn Neath and a pub at Ystradfellte

The Ystradfellte Waterfalls are a big attraction in these parts, particularly after heavy rainfall. They can, however, only be appreciated on foot as there are no bridleways or forestry tracks alongside the Afon Mellte, the river which tumbles down from the Brecon Beacons to join the River Neath.

The ride starts from Pontneddfechan, a village located on the very edge of the National Park, the boundary of which marks the great divide between the heavy industry to the south in the Neath and Cynon Valleys and the unspoilt woodland and moorland to the north. The ride climbs steeply to the east on an unusual stone staircase with fine views back down into the Neath Valley, dropping briefly onto the A4059 before turning north into the wooded valley of the Afon Mellte. The steep track out of Ystradfellte takes you up onto moorland and past an old lime kiln. A descent through forestry ending with a river crossing (be prepared for wet feet!) precedes a long downhill section on the old Roman road of Sarn Helen which used to run from Neath to Brecon. Unfortunately there is a missing section in our modern Rights of Way network about 1 mile north of Dyffryn Cellwen hence the two alternatives to the old Roman highway on this stretch. The long route suddenly drops you into a world of pylons and the old industrial past of South Wales before diving back into forestry down to Glyn Neath and the wooded, riverside section back to Pontneddfechan. The short route stays in the woodland to the north of the A4109 and uses quiet lanes to return to the start.

1 *From the car park at the eastern end of Pontneddfechan (GR 911079) follow the narrow, stone-based bridleway from the car park entrance, passing to the left of the dramatic cliff ahead. Steep climb (push) over limestone rock with ever more wonderful views behind you down the Vale of Neath. The gradient eases. At a fork of tracks by a wooden signpost* **bear R** *'Penderyn Bridleway'.*

2 *Climb to the brow then descend. At the road* **bear L**. *Go past church and the Red Lion PH.* **Keep bearing L** *on roads. At T-junction with main road (A4059)* **turn L**.

3 *After 1½ miles take the* **1st road to the L** *'Ystradfellte 2½'. Undulating section then steep climb. Shortly after the*

brow of the hill take the **1st road to the L** 'Waterfalls ½, Ystradfellte 1'.

4 At the New Inn in Ystradfellte **bear L then immediately R** onto no through road. Climb steeply. At X-roads at the end of the tarmac (with Tyle Farm signposted to the right) go **SA** to continue steeply uphill on broad, enclosed track.

5 At gate by wooden signpost continue **SA** alongside wall to the right then after 100 yards, as the wall turns sharp right continue **SA** on obvious grassy track. Follow this fine track passing through a metal gate in an immaculate section of drystone walling and past an old lime kiln. The track becomes enclosed. At T-junction with the road **turn L**.

6 After 1 mile **ignore** a right turn by 'Blaen Llia' Forestry Commission. After 400 yards **turn L** sharply back on yourself through gate onto forestry track. Climb then fast descent.

7 **Wet feet!** Cross the river onto the track opposite. Climb. At T-junction with the old Roman Road of Sarn Helen **turn L**.

8 Follow this stone-based track for 4 miles. One rough/stony ¾ mile section. Several deep puddles, some rideable, some not!

9 At road **bear R*** (in effect SA). **Although it would appear from the map that Sarn Helen continues, the track deteriorates then disappears and there is no continuous right of way, hence this lane diversion to Dyffryn Cellwen.** After 2 miles, at T-junction by triangle of grass **turn L**.

***(Short cut**. At the road **turn L** onto forestry track. After ½ mile take the **1st broad forestry track to the L** and continue in the same direction. **Ignore** turns to right and left. At T-junction with minor lane **turn L**. Steep descent, steep climb. At T-junction **turn R**. After 2 miles, at the bottom of the hill at the start of Pontneddfechan **turn L** sharply back on yourself by the Craig y Ddinas Hotel to return to the start)*.

10 *Full route. After 1¹/₂ miles, at X-roads with main road (A4109) go* **SA** *'Dyffren Cellwen'. After 300 yards* **turn L** *onto gravel track crossing a small wooden bridge. Follow around the left hand edge of the pond then* **bear L** *away from the pond at the far left hand corner.*

11 *Through several gates. At T-junction with pylons running straight ahead* **bear L** *to join tarmac road parallel with power lines.*

12 *Easily missed. climb to brow of hill. Tarmac turns to track. On fast descent* **take the first major track (wide forestry road) to the left by a wooden post.** *Follow blue arrows into the wood then shortly take the first track steeply downhill to the right.*

13 *Very steep descent. At T-junction with tarmac* **turn R** *downhill. At next T-junction, with the main road through Glyn Neath,* **turn L**.

14 *At traffic lights* **SA** *'Pontneddfechan'.* ***** *Follow the road beneath the bridge carrying the A465 dual carriageway, cross the river then climb. At the end of the row of houses on the left take the* **1st road to the L then immediately L** *again. Follow the track to the right past the playground.*

  * (Wet weather/winter alternative. Shortly after the traffic lights, **fork L** *onto the B4242 'Pontneddfechan'. After 1 mile go past Angel Inn and Tourist Information Centre. Shortly,* **bear R** *by the Craig y Ddinas Hotel and follow back to the start).*

15 *Full route. Go* **SA** *through gate past stone barn. Descend towards the river then follow the main (upper) track parallel with the river. Where the broad stone track ends* **bear R** *along the right hand field edge, parallel with the woodland to the right. (One stile to cross).*

16 *The track improves and passes beneath the A465. At T-junction with road* **turn L** *to return to the start.*

THE SIX RESERVOIR CHALLENGE IN THE BEACONS NORTH OF MERTHYR TYDFIL

DISTANCE
32 miles (51 kms)

TIME
6 hours

GRADE
Strenuous

TERRAIN
A bit of everything! Forestry, moorland, broadleaf woodland, reservoirs, high mountain pass, minor roads, railway paths, the outskirts of Merthyr Tydfil

HILLS AND HIGHPOINTS
1st climb ▲ 425 ft (130 mts) near the start from the end of Llwyn-on Reservoir south through the forest
2nd climb ▲ 1310 ft (400 mts) from Merthyr Tydfil to the pass beneath Fan y Big
3rd climb ▲ 625 ft (190 mts) up the old coach road to Storey Arms
Highest point ▲ 1965 feet (599 mts) at the pass beneath Pen y Fan
Total ascent ▲ 3860 ft (1175 mts)

START
Garwnant Forest Centre, 5 miles north of Merthyr Tydfil on the A470, just past Llwyn-on Reservoir (GR 003131)

PARKING
Garwnant Forest Centre car park

NEAREST RAILWAY
Merthyr Tydfil (2 miles south of the route)

REFRESHMENTS
Tea shop at the Garwnant Forest Centre
Pubs just off the route in Merthyr Tydfil, Vaynor, Pontsticil

The longest, if not the toughest circular ride in the book, the route embraces a whole range of changing scenery, from the old industrial town of Merthyr Tydfil to a high pass beneath the highest mountain in all of South Wales. In between are railway paths, forestry, moorland, an old coach road, broadleaf woodland, six reservoirs and sheep-grazed pasture.

The Forest Centre at Garwnant has a fine coffee shop to look forward to upon your return. The first climb starts soon after the end of the first reservoir, conveniently avoiding the busy A470. The new bypass is crossed on the descent into Merthyr Tydfil. The railway path (the Taff Trail) is a real delight, climbing steadily through broadleaf woodland towards the Brecon Beacons. Three more reservoirs are passed as the climb continues first on tarmac then on track up towards the high pass between Cribyn and Fan y Big. It is worth leaving this ride for a day with good visibility as the views are magnificent, as indeed is the descent to the north down into the network of lanes lying south of Brecon. Parts of the descent are technical and you may choose to stop and admire the views to give your arms time to rest and your wheels a chance to cool down.

Several miles on tiny quiet lanes take you to the start of the next offroad section - a long gentle climb up the old Brecon to Merthyr Tydfil coach road alongside a very fine drystone wall. The minimum time is spent on the busy A470 before diving off into forestry. There is a 1/2 mile section which will be boggy in the winter or after prolonged rain but before long you are back on solid ground for a wonderful fast descent back to the start.

1 *From the Garwnant Forest Centre (GR 003131) follow the exit signs back downhill. At T-junction with minor road* **turn sharp R** *(ie* **do not** *cross bridge). At the end of the reservoir* **bear R** *(in effect SA) on the right hand of two roads, signposted 'Taff Trail, Merthyr Tydfil'.*

2 *Steep road climb. Pass through farm.* **Ignore** *a right turn ('No bikes. Private') then on a sharp right hand bend at the start of the forestry,* **ignore** *a left turn ('No bikes. Walkers Taff Trail'). Follow the main forestry track as it swings sharp left uphill (GR004101). After further 1/2 mile climbing* **bear L** *(in effect SA) (GR 009097).*

3 *Superb descent. At fork of tracks by farm buildings* **bear R** *through gate. Descend*

steeply on tarmac. At T-junction with concrete road, just before the new A470 **turn L** *through bridlegate (blue arrow). Descend to pass under the new road and follow track round to the right, climbing parallel to the A470. The track turns to tarmac.*

4 *Go past a cemetery, descend steeply, pass beneath road bridge, cross bridge over river, then beneath railway viaduct. Climb steeply and go past the Cefn Coed Working Men's Club.* **Ignore** *turns to right and left.*

5 *At X-roads with the main road, at the end of Old Chapel Road* **turn L onto High Street then 1st R** *onto Old Drill Hall Road 'Taff Trail'. Take the narrow path between walls just to the left of the churchyard.*

6 *Follow the railway path for 3 miles. At the large metal barrier at the end of the railway path* **turn R then L** *onto road to continue in the same direction.* **Ignore** *a left turn then after 1/2 mile take the* **1st road to the R** *'Taff Trail'.*

7 *Leave the Taff Trail just before it crosses the dam for the Pontsticil Reservoir,* **bearing R** *(in effect SA) along the right hand side of the lake.* **Fork R** *at the sailing centre and follow the narrow path alongside the railway track.*

8 *At T-junction with the road with a disused railway bridge to your right* **bear L***. Follow lane across the dam between the two reservoirs then around the edge of Pontsticil Reservoir. After 400 yds take the* **1st road to the R** *'Talybont 81/2'.*

9 *After 3 miles (and 1 mile after crossing river)* **fork R** *onto track signposted 'No vehicles except 1-31 March, 1 Sept-15 October'.*

10 *Climb 590 ft (180 mts) over 21/2 miles. Superb views. Steep descent, technical at the start.*

11 *Track turns to tarmac and continues to descend steeply. Cross stream, start climbing and take the* **1st road to the L***, to continue climbing. After 3/4 mile take the*

next road L *(shortly after passing a turn to 'Cantref' to the right).*

12 *At fork of lanes (GR 031252)* **bear R.** *At T-junction by small bridge (GR 025253)* **turn L** *and follow the road round to the right.* **Ignore** *right turn. At X-roads (your priority) go* **SA***. At the next T-junction ('Penstar Farm' signposted ahead)* **turn L***.*

13 *After ³/₄ mile, at the next junction (GR 002249)* **bear L** *then follow the road round to the right.* **Ignore** *farm entrances to right and left. Descend to cross stream. Short climb, then on right hand bend by a stone house called 'Old Glanrhyd'* **turn L** *onto no through road signposted 'Storey Arms'.*

14 *Long steady climb on the old Brecon-Merthyr Tydfil coach road alongside a very fine drystone wall. At T-junction with the main A470 by a telephone box* **turn L.**

15 *After 1¹/₂ miles on this busy road, at the end of the reservoir* **1st R** *onto the A4059 'Neath'. Cross bridge then* **1st track L** *into forestry 'Taff Trail'. Go over a stile. Boggy section towards the end. Cross a second stile.*

16 *Follow the main track climbing gently for 1 mile then gently downhill for 2 miles. At T-junction (GR 000132)* **turn L then shortly L again** *to return to the start.*

HIGH MOUNTAIN PASS THROUGH THE BRECON BEACONS WEST OF TALYBONT

DISTANCE
19 miles (30 kms)

TIME
3¹/₂ hours

GRADE
Strenuous

TERRAIN
Forestry, moorland, reservoir

HILLS AND HIGHPOINTS
*One major climb ▲ 1150 ft (350 mts)
over 3 miles to reach the pass beneath
Fan y Big
Highest point ▲ 1965 ft (599 mts)
at the pass beneath Fan y Big
Total ascent ▲ 1870 ft (570 mts)*

START
*The Post Office/stores in Talybont on Usk,
on the B4558 between Crickhowell
and Brecon*

PARKING
On the road near to the Post Office/stores

NEAREST RAILWAY
Merthyr Tydfil, 7 miles south of the route

REFRESHMENTS
*The Star PH, White Hart PH
Stores in Talybont on Usk*

*One of several rides starting
in or near Talybont, this one
explores the high pass through
the Beacons in the reverse
direction from Ride 6 (The Six
Reservoir Challenge) so that
you are faced with a much
steeper climb but a
longer descent.*

The ride spends the first seven miles on road; after leaving the B4558, most of this tarmac section is on tiny, quiet lanes with next to no traffic and magnificent views of the challenge that awaits you away to the south with the ridge of the Brecon Beacons filling the horizon. The broad stony track stretches ahead and you will probably have to walk a good part of the ascent.
Savour the views at the summit of the pass and feast your eyes on the delights that lie ahead: the long descent down into the valley of Taf Fechan with the Upper Neuadd Reservoir down to your right. You barely touch tarmac at the bottom before you bear off again onto track through Tal Fechan Forest. After a ³/4 mile climb on road you are now set up for the dream descent down into Talybont, the perfect downhill gradient as far as the end of the reservoir. Here you have a choice: follow the waymarked Taff Trail on road, continuing downhill into Talybont, or for an offroad finish, a short climb from the end of the reservoir joins you up with a bridleway right back into the heart of the village.

1 *With back to the Post Office/stores in Talybont* **turn R** *along the B4558 towards Brecon.*

2 *After 2 miles, shortly after the 'Pencelli' sign at the start of the village, opposite Pencelli Castle Caravan Park* **turn L** *onto road signposted 'Plas Pencelli, Taff Trail'.*

3 **Ignore** *several left turns. After 1¹/2 miles, at T-junction by telephone box and church in Llanfrynach* **turn L then after 150 yds turn L** *'Cantref 1¹/4, Taff Trail'.*

4 *After 1 mile take the* **1st road L** *by small triangle of grass 'Pentwyn' then after ¹/2 mile take the* **1st road to the R**.

5 *Cross two streams in quick succession.* **Ignore** *the no through road to the left. Shortly, take the* **next road L**, *sharply back on yourself. Pass through farm.* **Ignore** *a right turn, descend to cross another stream then gird your loins for the BIG climb! 1150 ft (350 mts) over 3 miles.*

6 *Steep climb on tarmac then track to the gate. The gradient continues steep then eases for the middle section of the climb before the final push up to the pass.*

7 *Enjoy the fabulous descent, with one steep drop and climb out of a side stream. At T-junction with road* **bear L then shortly L** *again onto track.*

8 *At next T-junction with road* **turn L** *to cross cattle grid then climb steeply.* **Ignore** *first right turn at the brow. Take the* **next R** *'Taff Trail. Forestry Commission Tal y Bont'.*

9 *Heavenly descent over 6 miles.* **Do not cross dam**. *Stay on the right hand side of the reservoir/river.*

10 *¹/2 mile after passing the dam* **bear R** *uphill at fork 'Taff Trail'. Climb then descend on the Taff Trail. At T-junction with the B4558 in Talybont* **turn L** *to return to the Post Office.*

THREE RESERVOIRS
SOUTHWEST OF TALYBONT

DISTANCE
Short route 16 miles (26 kms)
Long Route 20 miles (32 kms)

TIME
Short route 3 hours
Long Route 4 hours

GRADE
Strenuous

TERRAIN
Moorland, forestry, reservoirs

HILLS AND HIGHPOINTS
1st climb: ▲ 1265 ft (395 mts)
from Talybont to the highpoint above
Talybont Reservoir, most of the hard work
is on a quiet lane
2nd climb ▲ 360 ft (110 mts)
from the reservoir up to the start of the
Talybont forestry section
Highest point ▲ 1675 feet (510 mts)
at the pass / fork of tracks above Dolygaer
Total ascent ▲ 2130 ft (650 mts)

START
The Post Office / Stores in Talybont on Usk,
on the B4558, 6 miles southeast of Brecon

PARKING
Near the Post Office in Talybont

NEAREST RAILWAY
Merthyr Tydfil, 7 miles south of the route

REFRESHMENTS
The Star PH, White Hart PH, stores
in Talybont on Usk

Talybont on Usk is one of the best centres for offroad cycling in the region with routes heading off in all directions. It lies on the Taff Trail which runs from Cardiff to Brecon and is a small, attractive village with good pubs and a village store.

From the heart of the village the ride climbs steeply on tarmac to high above the Talybont Reservoir which nestles below in a bowl of wooded slopes. At the top of the climb you have two options – the shorter route descends on a wide RUPP (Road Used as a Public Path) dropping down through woodland to Dolygaer at the end of Pentwyn Reservoir. The longer route stays higher on the moorland and drops gently then more steeply to the southern end of Pontsticil Reservoir. The two routes join and climb steeply on road before the six mile dream descent down the Taff Trail back to Talybont. The descent is so good that it can also be found in two other rides – the Talybont Forestry Ride (Ride 9) and the West of Talybont Ride (Ride 7).

1 With your back to the Post Office and stores in Talybont **turn L** past the two pubs. Pass beneath the old railway bridge and take the **next lane to the R**.

2 Climb steeply with reservoir views opening up to your right. After 3 miles, towards the top of the climb, **ignore** a left turn to Bwlchywaun (signpost on gate).

3 Tarmac turns to track and starts descending. At T-junction with wide forestry track **bear L. (For a short route turn R** here for a fast descent back to the start**)**.

4 At fork of tracks (GR 100175) **bear R** at sign with Taff Trail logo (two arches). **Do not bear left on the good forestry track with cattle grid just ahead.**

5 Steady then steep climb on stone surface with ever better views down to Talybont Reservoir. At fork of tracks at the top of the climb by a three-way wooden signpost **turn R*** 'Dolygaer' and follow the main left hand track.

* (For extra loop, see 'Alternative Route').

6 Follow this track over an undulating moorland section then drop to cross gully and enter forestry via gate. Stony woodland descent. Emerge at the outdoor activity centre at Dolygaer where track turns to tarmac.

7 Follow tarmac lane across the dam between the two reservoirs then around the edge of Pontsticil Reservoir. After 400 yds take the **1st road to the R** 'Talybont 8$\frac{1}{2}$'. Climb. After 1 mile take the **next road to the R** 'Aber 6$\frac{1}{2}$, Talybont 7$\frac{1}{2}$'.

8 Descend then climb steeply. **Ignore** the first right turn at the brow. Take the **next R** 'Taff Trail. Forestry Commission Tal y Bont'.

9 Heavenly descent over 6 miles. **Do not cross dam.** Stay on the right hand side of the reservoir / river. $\frac{1}{2}$ mile after passing the dam **bear R** uphill at fork 'Taff Trail'.

10 Follow Taff Trail signs down to Talybont, crossing bridges over the old railway line then the canal. At T-junction with the road **turn L** to return to the Post Office.

* Alternative Route to Pontsticil village

A From the three-way wooden signpost at the top of the climb (GR 090161) follow signs for Pontsticil. Soon after the fork the track turns to grass. The last section near the quarry will be boggy in parts, particularly in the winter months or after prolonged rain.

B At the gravel track by the quarry **turn R**. Go round a sharp left hand then right hand bend. Briefly join a concrete road. **Easy to miss**. after 200 yards, opposite a gravel track to the left **bear R** onto a faint grassy track parallel to the road.

C Fine grassy descent then some stream crossings which break the rhythm. Gentle climb for $\frac{3}{4}$ mile. Fine views over Pontsticil Reservoir.

D **Extremely easy to miss!** (GR 068123) On contouring track, soon after the end of the small deciduous woodland to the right and more or less opposite the south end of the forestry plantation on the other side of the reservoir, **turn R downhill on a faint, narrow grass track,** aiming for the pointed tower at the end of the reservoir. This will bring you to a metal gate in the wall. I have started a cairn where the faint track leaves the main track. If you find the cairn, please add to it!

E *Through the metal gate and **bear diagonally L** downhill through field following the line of the old trees to a bridlegate in the corner. Continue in the same direction (heading away from the reservoir at this point). Pass beneath railway bridge, cross two gravel tracks to continue steeply downhill. At T-junction with road **turn R**.*

F *Follow Taff Trail signs to cross the road over the dam. At T-junction **turn sharply R** 'Talybont 10¹/₂'. After ¹/₂ mile **1st L** 'Taff Trail / National Cycle Network 8'.*

G *Climb through forestry, descend to cross bridge over stream. Climb then descend to the road. At T-junction with road **turn L** then shortly follow the road sharply left 'Talybont 8 ¹/₂'. Rejoin the route at second half of Instruction 7 'Climb. After 1 mile...'*

A FORESTRY CIRCUIT OF TALYBONT RESERVOIR

DISTANCE
12 miles (19 km)

TIME
2 hours

GRADE
Moderate

TERRAIN
Reservoir, forestry, all-weather tracks

HILLS AND HIGHPOINTS
1st climb ▲ 890 ft (270 mts)
on forestry tracks
2nd climb ▲ 590 ft (180 mts)
steeply on road
Highest point ▲ 1410 ft (430 mts)
at the top of the steep road climb
Total ascent ▲ 1480 ft (450 mts)

START
Car park at GR 099197, 3 miles south of
Talybont on Usk on the minor road
signposted 'Talybont Reservoir'

PARKING
Car park at GR 099197

NEAREST RAILWAY
Merthyr Tydfil, 8 miles south of the route

REFRESHMENTS
Lots of choice in Talybont on Usk

*This ride uses one of the best
sections of the Taff Trail, the
long and magnificent forestry
descent on the course of an old
tramway from high above
Talybont Reservoir down to its
shores at its northern end.
However, no descent of such
high calibre is easily won.*

There are two climbs (with almost 1500 ft of ascent) to get you to the top. The first starts right opposite the car park and takes you high above the valley with fine views north to the dramatic ridge of Waun Rydd. The first fast descent of the day is on forestry roads and drops you back on to the valley road. Beware of the wooden barrier across the end of the track just by the road! You go round a bend at warp factor three and there is this large wooden gate blocking your way. You have been warned! The climb on road is very steep and made much less pleasant if the road is busy. If you can, try to avoid fine summer weekends (except early morning and evening) when traffic is likely to be at its heaviest. Enjoy the views at the top before turning east for the glorious descent back to the start. The distinct advantage of this route is that it is rideable all year round and will not be affected by rain and mud.

1 *From the car park on the west side of Talybont Reservoir (GR 099197) cross the road onto the Forestry Commission track opposite. Climb steadily. The gradient eases shortly after a track joins from the right.*

2 *For a short route, soon after the track starts descending,* **keep an eye out for a track sharply back down to your left.** *Follow this down to the road then* **turn L** *to return to the start.*

3 *For the full route, continue SA, climbing with fabulous views of the Waun Rydd ridge to the right.*

4 *Continue over the brow of the hill, descend.* **Ignore** *one left and one right turn. This is a fast descent but* **be warned!** *There is a wooden barrier at the bottom so you will need to be able to stop quickly when you see it! At the road* **turn R.**

5 *Climb steeply for 1 mile (this section may be busy at the weekends/in summer). At the brow of the hill* **turn L** *onto Forestry Commission track signposted 'Taff Trail'.*

6 *Glorious descent over 6 miles. At the end of the reservoir* **turn L, then shortly at**

T-junction turn L again to return to the start.

▶ *Ride 6*

▶ *Ride 9*

▶ *Ride 7*

Ride 8 ◄

Ride 10 ◄

Ride 9 ◄
Ride 8 ►

▶ *Ride 9*

▶ *Ride 11*

▶ *Ride 11*

◀ *Ride 11*

Ride 12 ◀

Ride 14 ◀

Ride 14 ◀

10

THE VALLEY OF DYFFRYN CRAWNON SOUTHWEST OF LLANGYNIDR

DISTANCE
15 miles (24 kms)
TIME
3 hours
GRADE
Moderate

TERRAIN
Quiet dead-end lane, steep forestry climb, fine views, forestry tracks. Some sections of bridleway are very rough

HILLS AND HIGHPOINTS
One major climb ▲ 1115 ft (340 mts)
from the start to the treeline
Highest point ▲ 1510 ft (460 mts)
Total ascent ▲ 1480 ft (450 mts)

START
The car park in Llangynidr which lies halfway between Abergavenny and Brecon on the B4558, parallel with the A40. (GR 155195)

PARKING
The car park in Llangynidr

NEAREST RAILWAY
Rhymney, 6 miles south of the route at Instruction 4

REFRESHMENTS
Two pubs in Llangynidr

Llangynidr is one of those villages that lies just above an invisible line that separates the industrialised valleys to the south that are still recovering from the demise of the coal and steel industry and the farming land of hedgerows and sheep pasture untouched by heavy industry which lie to the north.

The social problems brought about by high unemployment in the valleys can be seen by the burnt-out cars on the track near to this dividing line. There can be few areas in the country where the juxaposed contrast is so great between industrial scars and breathtakingly beautiful countryside. The ride climbs gently on the delightful lane running along the Crawnon valley before turning steeply uphill up through the forestry to the head of the valley and the watershed of the River Usk. For a mile at the top the going is slow and stony although you are well compensated by fabulous views back down the valley. The track improves through woodland and as far as Bwlch Y Waun Farm. Beyond the farm there are some rougher sections on the descent until reaching the road and enjoying the fast and furious tarmac descent back down to Llangynidr.

NB. This is a ride that would also be worth trying in reverse.

1 *Exit the car park and* **turn R** *onto Dyffryn Road. Follow the road past the Red Lion PH and the church, following signs for Dyffryn Crawnon.*

2 *After 3 miles go past the telephone box in the hamlet of Wern. After a further 2 miles, keep an eye out for a farm on the right called Pyrgad (wooden signpost nailed to tree). Just past the farm leave the road and* **turn L** *through gate onto track signposted 'Pyrgad Campsite'.*

3 *Steep climb, passing a waterfall (and probably some burnt-out cars). Near the top, soon after climbing above the tree line, follow the track around a right hand hairpin bend. At T-junction with tarmac* **turn R** *then after 200 yards* **bear R** *onto broad stone track.*

4 *Superb views down the valley.* **Easily missed.** *200 yards after the end of the pine trees to your right* **leave the stone track and bear R** *alongside the fence on a grassy track.*

5 *After a short, easy section, the next mile will be slow and only rideable in parts although very beautiful. In addition there are two stiles to negotiate. Once in the wood the track improves and is 90% rideable.*

6 *At T-junction with a wide forestry track* **bear L, then keep bearing/forking R** *and climbing. Track turns to tarmac.* **Ignore** *a footpath/track to the right signposted 'Bryn Melyn'.*

7 *After a short descent take the* **next R** *through a gate in the stone wall onto a tarmac lane. 'Bwlchywaun' sign on the gate. 'No through road' wooden signpost.*

8 *Through farm and gate with blue arrow onto track, at times rough and muddy. Several gates. At a fork of tracks by a barn go through the right hand gate. At T-junction with the road* **bear L.** *Climb briefly then fast descent on tarmac. At T-junction with the B4558* **turn R** *and return to the car park in Llangynidr.*

11

ABERGAVENNY AND THE CIRCUIT OF THE BLORENGE

DISTANCE
14 miles (22 kms)

TIME
3 hours

GRADE
Moderate

TERRAIN
Railway path through woodland, minor lane network, track over moorland and through woodland nature reserve with magnificent views

HILLS AND HIGHPOINTS
1st climb ▲ 1500 ft (460 mts) from the start of the railway path in Llanfoist up to the B4246 near to Pen-ffordd-goch Pond at the top of the hill
2nd climb ▲ 360 ft (110 mts) from near to the pond in the Punchbowl Nature Reserve to the road
Highest point: ▲ 1640 feet (500 mts) just to the west of Blorenge
Total ascent ▲ 2000 ft (610 mts)

START
The Tourist Information Centre/bus station/car park in Abergavenny, near to the castle

PARKING
The Tourist Information Centre/bus station/car park in Abergavenny

NEAREST RAILWAY
Abergavenny

REFRESHMENTS
Plenty of choice in Abergavenny. Pubs in Llanfoist

This ride links together Abergavenny via the railway path from Llanfoist to a circuit of Blorenge to provide a varied and challenging circuit right on the edge of the great divide between the industrialised valleys of South Wales and the rural character of mid-Wales.

To the north lies the picturesque patchwork of fields and hedgerows; the slag heaps to the southwest of Blorenge mark the edge of the mining industry to the south. The ride shows how Abergavenny can be seen as the true gateway to the upland areas of South and Mid-Wales. Having left Abergavenny from the back of the castle and crossed the ancient stone bridge over the River Usk, you soon come to Llanfoist where you join the fine broad gravel track climbing steadily through woodland along the course of the old railway line. Views of Blorenge open up as you climb the network of tiny lanes and soon you arrive at the dramatic sight of the black mining spoils poised like a menacing wave threatening to pour over the hill and down into the Usk Valley. There is no right of way for bikes to the summit of Blorenge–the (easily missed) bridleway swings downhill and contours around the base of the hill and below the Punchbowl Nature Reserve before a last climb back up to the road. A fast tarmac descent leads back to the outward route in Llanfoist.

NB. This is a route that could also be enjoyed in the opposite direction.

1 With your back to the Tourist Information Centre/bus station/long stay car park in the centre of Abergavenny **turn R then L** onto Mill Street (no through road). Shortly **bear R** signposted 'Mill Street Industrial Estate' **then R** again. Join a concrete path and descend towards metal barrier. Follow the path alongside the river.

2 Cross the River Usk via the old stone bridge. Immediately after the Bridge Inn cross the road onto lowered pavement and follow the pavement round to the right. Cross the next road via crossing point onto opposite pavement (by a petrol station), **turn R** and follow this pavement/cyclepath through metal barrier and under viaduct into Llanfoist village.

3 At X-roads by the Llanfoist Inn **turn R** then shortly after the car saleroom and a street called The Cedars on the right **take**

the next narrow tarmac track to the R (signposted as a 'No through road'). Immediately **turn L** onto the old railway path.

4 After 2 miles, at road crossing go **SA**, past the Old Govilon Station.
Pass beneath a railway bridge then leave the railway path via a small car parking area on your right, **turning L** onto the minor lane. Climb then shortly **fork L** crossing the bridge over the railway path. Climb steeply, go through a gate then 300 yards after the second cottage on the right **turn sharply L** by a large boulder wall on to a grass and stone track.

5 Magnificent views north and northeast to the Sugar Loaf, Ysgyryd Fawr and Black Mountains. Steep then steady climb. At T-junction with the B4246 **turn L then R** onto the track around the edge of the lake signposted 'Llanfoist 4.8 kms'. At the far end of the lake by a stone map/plinth cross a small bridge over the stream and **turn R** onto a grassy track, climbing gently.

6 **Extremely easy to miss!** Follow this contouring path for 1 mile. Shortly after crossing one of the several rocky 10 yard sections along the path, keep a sharp eye out for **a flat stone to the left of the path painted with a blue marker indicating a small faint track descending to the left** (almost due north, towards the distinctive table-top shape of Sugar Loaf). I have started a cairn here – if you find the cairn, please add to it! If you find yourself in a grassy cutting with earthbanks on either side you have gone too far. Retrace your steps.

7 There are a few short, unrideable sections at the start of the descent but the path soon becomes a fine, smooth track down the fern-covered hillside.
At T-junction with grass and stone track by the conifer woodland **bear R**.

8 Follow this obvious track, passing through the Woodland Trust Nature Reserve. The track climbs steeply after the pond then levels out. At T-junction with the road **turn L** downhill for a fast descent. At T-junction with another lane **turn L**, for another fast descent *under a canopy of trees. At T-junction with the B4269* **turn L** *(this is a busier road).*

9 *At the T-junction in Llanfoist* **turn L then R** *onto The Cutting to rejoin the outward route back to Abergavenny. Cross the bridge over the River Usk* **then turn immediately R** *onto the track alongside the river towards the castle.*

12

VALLEY AND MOUNTAIN VIEWS FROM THE IRON AGE HILL FORT NORTH OF BWLCH

DISTANCE
Short route 8 miles (13 kms)
Full route 13 miles (21 kms)

TIME
Short route 1¹/₂ hours
Full route 2 hours

GRADE
Moderate

TERRAIN
Arable land, broadleaf and conifer woodland, hedgerows, grass and gorse hilltop, red soil, valley of the River Usk, views of Black Mountains and Brecon Beacons

HILLS AND HIGHPOINTS
1st climb ▲ 720 ft (220 mts)
to the top of the hill fort
2nd climb ▲ 240 ft (73 mts)
from Pennorth to the top of the second hill
Highest point ▲ 1280 feet (390 mts)
at the top of the hill fort
Total ascent ▲ short route 820 ft (250 mts)
▲ long route 1280 ft (390 mts)

START
The junction of the B4560 and the A40 in Bwlch, between Brecon and Abergavenny

PARKING
No specific car park. Please use common sense and consideration

NEAREST RAILWAY
Abergavenny, 13 miles east of Bwlch

REFRESHMENTS
New Inn, Morning Star PH
Farmers Arms PH
Black Cock Inn, Llanfihangel Tal-y-llyn
two stores in Bwlch

This is a short ride much easier than those all around it but with some magnificent views notwithstanding. Unlike many of the higher rides this passes through arable farmland, with ploughed fields of red soil either side of the track.

The start from Bwlch may seem a bit convoluted but it avoids a dangerous right turn on a blind bend of the busy A40. Once offroad the narrow bridleway climbs between hedgerows and banks covered with wildflowers in the spring and early summer. Views open up as the track climbs and emerges into the grassland and gorse. To the east lies Mynydd Llangorse, Mynydd Troed and the Black Mountains. To the west lie the Brecon Beacons and the steep escarpment of Pen y Fan, at 2907 ft (886 mts), the highest mountain in South Wales. The River Usk snakes through the valley, a chequered patchwork of red earth, green grass, and brown moorland. After the descent from the hill fort you have a choice of returning to Bwlch or doing a second loop which takes in the Black Cock Inn at Llanfihangel Tal-y-llyn.

WARNING! This route will be very muddy in winter or after prolonged rain.

1 From the west end of Bwlch take the B4560 northwards away from the A40, signposted 'Llangorse'. After 1/2 mile take the **1st road to the L** 'Pennorth 3 1/4' then after 1/4 mile **turn 1st L** onto the lane by the stone-built 'Saw Mill Cottages'.
At the top of the climb, on a sharp left hand bend, **immediately after the drive to Middlewood Farm turn R** onto narrow track 'Bridleway.'

2 Long steady ascent on a narrow track. This section will be muddy in winter / after prolonged rain. Go past small ruin then **bear L** uphill between lines of old trees. Continue in the same direction to the left of a small plantation to reach the top of the hill for superb views, particularly down across the Usk Valley away towards Pen y Fan.

3 Good descent, at times narrow. Muddy in winter. The track soon broadens to tractor width. As the main track swings sharply right downhill **bear L.**

4 **Short route**. At T-junction with lane **turn R** and follow this lane for 3 1/2 miles. At T-junction with B4560 **turn R** to return to the start.

5 **Long route** (with possible pub stop in Llanfihangel Tal-y-Llyn). At T-junction with lane **turn L** then 1/4 mile after passing telephone box in Pennorth and shortly after passing a modern house called Glaslyn on the right, take the **next R** onto a bridleway between two tarmac drives.

6 Steady climb past a white-topped mast and on to the brow of the hill. Fine views of Pen y Fan to the left and the Black Mountains to the right.

7 Descend. At T-junction with the road **turn R**. At next T-junction **turn R*** 'Pennorth'.

 * (Turn L here for the Black Cock Inn in Llanfihangel Tal-y-Llyn, **turn R** in the village for the pub).

8 At the T-junction in Pennorth **turn L** 'Bwlch 3 3/4'.

9 After 3 1/2 miles, at T-junction with B4560 **turn R** 'Bwlch 1/2' to return to the start.

13

PENGENFFORDD TO BWLCH VIA MYNYDD LLANGORSE AND CEFN MOEL

DISTANCE
15 miles (24 kms)

TIME
3 hours

GRADE
Strenuous

TERRAIN
Sheep pasture, moorland and a small patch of forestry. Hedgerows, stone walls and broad tracks, some used by pony trekking centres

HILLS AND HIGHPOINTS
1st climb ▲ 560 ft (170 mts)
exceedingly steep push up onto Mynydd Llangorse
2nd climb ▲ 395 ft (120 mts)
from the B4560 past Treholford
Highest point ▲ 1510 feet (460 mts)
on Mynydd Llangorse
Total ascent ▲ 1740 ft (530 mts)

START
The Castle Inn, Pengenffordd, on the A479 between Crickhowell and Talgarth. (3 miles south of Talgarth)

PARKING
In the pub car park. It costs £1 and should be paid to the pub when you turn up. Please do not abuse this system, you will ruin it for everyone if you do

NEAREST RAILWAY
Abergavenny, 12 miles east of Bwlch

REFRESHMENTS
Castle Inn, Pengenffordd
New Inn, Morning Star PH
Farmers Arms PH
two stores in Bwlch

The first of three rides starting from the magnificently located Castle Inn at Pengenffordd, at the highpoint of the A479 to the south of Talgarth.

You could just as easily start this ride from Bwlch, to the west of Crickhowell and make the Castle Inn your lunchtime stop. To do this, start at the second half of Instruction no. 7 '...After ¼ mile heading west on the A40'. The ride is fairly straightforward and does not climb as high as the rides immediately to the east and west BUT there is one short, exceedingly steep push of 560 ft (170 mts) up the eastern side of Mynydd Llangorse. You have been warned! From the start, after a short climb from Pengenffordd the ride passes along the base of Mynydd Troed at the border between pasture and moorland. There are brief views of Llangorse Lake at the road crossing before a wonderful, gentle descent down Cwm Sorgwm with a backdrop of Pen Cerrig-calch at the southwestern corner of the Black Mountains. The infamous climb mentioned above follows next, soon rewarded by the best views of the day and, before long, the best descent on a broad and ever steeper track down into the village of Bwlch with three inns and two stores. After a couple of miles on the B4560, a second steep climb (shorter than the first!) takes you up to a path that contours along the western flank of Mynydd Llangorse with fine views of the lake. At several stages you will be cursing the pony trekking centres whose horses leave sections of the paths with incredibly frustrating corrugations or turn the path into a trough which is just too narrow to turn the pedals with ease. Don't despair– it does improve and before long you are back on the outward track on your return to the Castle Inn. There is a good chance that you will take a slightly different course on your return as there are several bridleways–no problem, all tracks lead to the Castle Inn!

1 *With your back to the Castle Inn, Pengenffordd (on the A479, 3 miles south of Talgarth),* **turn R towards Talgarth** *then 30 yards after the end of the car park* **bear R** *onto a track running parallel with the road between hedgerows. After 300 yards, with 'No through road' to the right,* **turn L**

across the main road and then through the farmyard.

2 *Follow the track round to the right past the barn then shortly* **turn L** *uphill towards a metal gate. At the second gate, at the end of the enclosed track go* **SA** *on grassy track.* **Ignore** *the path to the left which climbs steeply up onto Mynydd Troed. There are several paths which run parallel in the same direction, eventually they merge alongside a stone wall on the right.*

3 *Llangorse Lake comes into sight. The tracks split again, but as long as you aim towards the obvious ridge of Mynydd Llangorse looming ahead of you you can't go wrong. At the lane* **turn L then shortly R** *onto track.*

4 *Superb gentle descent with fine views of the ridge of Pen Cerrig-calch ahead. After 1½ miles, with the gate onto the road in sight,* **fork R** *to follow the fence around the field, soon* **forking R** *again and taking the exceedingly steep path to the top. (It will be worth it, honest!).*

5 *At the path junction shortly after the cairn* **bear R then soon fork L** *around the rim of the valley down to your left.* **Do not descend into the valley** *but continue* **SA** *across the back of the whaleback hill to join a path coming down from the summit which lies to your right.* **Bear L** *(GR 158256).*

6 *Follow the path alongside fence then wall. Panoramic views. The descent steepens. Join the road by a house and continue downhill.*

7 *At T-junction* **turn R**. *At the next T-junction (with the A40)* **turn R,** *(or* **turn L** *for refreshments at the New Inn or the Morning Star PH in Bwlch). After ¼ mile heading west on the A40 towards Brecon* **turn first R** *onto the B4560 'Llangorse'.*

8 *After 2 miles, descend to cross stream. Climb past a farm on the right then take the* **next lane to the R** *'Treholford'. Climb steeply. As the stone track swings left* towards a large house **bear R** through bridlegate 'Bridleway' and continue steeply uphill.

9 Go past a house and immediately **bear R** through gate and follow track alongside fence. Go past ruins, then a cottage, then across a field. Technical woodland descent. At X-roads with a wider forestry track go **SA**.

10 Exit forestry and follow the obvious track, corrugated by the hooves of trekking ponies. **Easily missed**, at fork of tracks soon after crossing a small stream **do not follow the track downhill** alongside the fence to the left **but bear R** on the contouring path.

11 The track becomes progressively more rideable. At the road, go **SA** through gate onto path to rejoin outward route.

12 By following the fence on the return trip you are likely to return a different way. No problem! As the road comes into sight, **bear R** on broad grass track 30 yards before the gate.

13 Follow this track through the farm, passing through several gates. Cross the main road then **turn R** onto the track running parallel with the road to return to the Castle Inn at Pengenffordd.

14

A CIRCUIT OF MYNYDD TROED AND CASTELL DINAS FROM PENGENFFORDD

DISTANCE
12 miles (20 kms)

TIME
3 hours

GRADE
Strenuous

TERRAIN
Moorland and wooded valleys, high mountain pass, sheep pasture and farm lanes

HILLS AND HIGHPOINTS
One major climb ▲ 1460 ft (445 mts) from the A479 at Pont Waun Fach to the mountain pass
Second climb ▲ 360 ft (110 mts) from the crossing of Rhiangoll stream to the second pass
Highest point ▲ 2025 ft (617 mts) at the first mountain pass
Total ascent ▲ 2400 ft (730 mts)

START
The Castle Inn, Pengenffordd, on the A479 between Crickhowell and Talgarth. (3 miles south of Talgarth)

PARKING
In the pub car park. It costs £1 and should be paid to the pub when you turn up. Please do not abuse this system, you will ruin it for everyone if you do

NEAREST RAILWAY
Builth Road is 12 miles NNW of Talgarth

REFRESHMENTS
Castle Inn, Pengenffordd

This ride shares the same start as Ride 13 but parts company at the bottom of the fine descent down Cwm Sorgwm. Whereas the other ride turns west on a steep ascent of Mynydd Llangorse this ride climbs east up to one of the real mountain biking crossroads in the Black Mountains.

DIRECTIONS *A circuit of Mynydd Troed and Castell Dinas from Pengenffordd*

At the cairn at 2025 ft (617 mts), not only should you enjoy fantastic views but you also have three excellent options: the first (the shortest) is a fast and technical descent down Rhiw Trumau; the second (the longest) is a chance to extend the ride to a real monster by linking with the Grwyne Fawr Ride (Ride 15) and following this in reverse, starting with the long, fine descent down Grwyne Fechan to Llanbedr; the third option, the one described below, maintains height for longer, and crosses a second grassy pass to the east of the atmospheric hill fort of Castell Dinas. A fast tarmac descent takes you back to the delights of the Castle Inn at Pengenffordd.

1 With your back to the Castle Inn, **turn R towards Talgarth then 30 yards after the end of the car park bear R** onto a track running parallel with the road between hedgerows. After 300 yards, with 'No through road' to the right, **turn L** across the main road and through the farmyard.

2 Follow the track round to the right past the barn then shortly **turn L** uphill towards a metal gate. At the second gate, at the end of the enclosed track go **SA** on grassy track, ignoring the path to the left which climbs steeply up onto Mynydd Troed. There are several paths which run parallel in the same direction, eventually they merge alongside a stone wall on the right.

3 Llangorse Lake comes into sight. The tracks split again, continue **SA** towards the obvious ridge of Mynydd Llangorse. At the lane **turn L then shortly R** onto track

4 Superb gentle descent with fine views of Pen Cerrig-calch ridge ahead. After 1¹/₂ miles, exit the gate onto the road and **turn L**. Descend steeply, pass through farm then climb. At T-junction with minor lane **turn R**.

5 At T-junction with main road (A479) by a telephone box **turn R then after 300 yds take the 1st lane L**. After ³/₄ mile, at X-roads of lanes by a triangle of grass go **SA then almost immediately bear R** onto steep stone track 'Bridleway'. (Start of the big push).

6 At T-junction with next lane **turn R**, cross cattle grid then shortly **bear L** onto steep track 'Bridleway'. Go through metal field gate then bridlegate, passing to the right of a concrete water tank.
Follow the main track steeply uphill, through a gap in the fence, continuing uphill towards the gap in the next fence/wall. **Turn L** along this second fence/wall and follow easier gradient to the cairn at the pass.

7 At the top 2025 ft (617 mts) by the cairn you have three choices of descent:

   a) **Go SA** to descend the other side to Llanbedr and do the Grwynne Fawr Ride in reverse (Ride 15).

   b) **Turn L** and take the steep, technical, fast descent down Rhiw Trumau back to the start.
   (Follow Ride 15, Instructions 14-15).

   c) **Bear L** onto the least distinct of the various tracks, soon **forking R** and contouring or gently climbing.
   This is the main route.

8 The track crosses several small streams. Pass to the left of the next large cairn and to the right of a 3rd cairn. The track becomes less distinct. **Keep bearing L**, losing height. You will cross a secondary valley then the stream/river in the main valley.
You are aiming for a small barn/shed in a corner of the field at the bottom of the valley (up the valley from Grafog, the last of the outlying farms).

9 Cross the river in the main valley and soon **fork R** uphill on obvious, broad, grassy track aiming for the 'pass' on the ridge. Fantastic views. Follow the broad track downhill then **bear L** more steeply downhill towards bridlegate in fence.

10 At T-junction with road **turn L** through gate onto broad stone track, which passes to the north of Castell Dinas. The track turns to tarmac. Fast descent. At T-junction with the main road (A479) **turn L** to return to the start.

▶ *Ride 15*

▶ *Ride 17*

▶ *Ride 16*

Ride 18 ◀

Ride 17 ◀

Ride 18 ◀

Ride 18 ▶

Ride 19 ◀

Ride 19 ◀

Ride 20 ◀

15

GRWYNE FAWR AND GRWYNE FECHAN
THE CLASSIC BLACK MOUNTAINS CIRCUIT

DISTANCE
25 miles (40 kms)

TIME
6 hours

GRADE
Strenuous

TERRAIN
High moorland, woodland, pasture

HILLS AND HIGHPOINTS
1st climb ▲ 1150 ft (350 mts)
from Ffosrhys (GR 188329) to the
top of the moorland
2nd climb ▲ 1530 ft (470 mts)
over 7 miles from Llanbedr to the
second pass at the top of Rhiw Trumau
Highpoints ▲ (1) 2265 feet (690 mts)
above the Grwyne Fawr Reservoir
▲ (2) 2025 feet (617 mts)
at the top of the valley of the Grwyne Fechan
Total ascent ▲ 4000 ft (1220 mts)

START
The Castle Inn, Pengenffordd, on the A479
between Crickhowell and Talgarth.
(3 miles south of Talgarth)

PARKING
In the pub car park. It costs £1 and should
be paid to the pub when you turn up. Please
do not abuse this system, you will ruin it for
everyone else if you do

This is the toughest ride in the book with two of the most sustained climbs, the first of which is a steep and stony push rewarded not only by magnificent views but also by a very fine eight mile descent.

NEAREST RAILWAY
Abergavenny, 6 miles from the route
near to Partrishow

REFRESHMENTS
Castle Inn, Pengenffordd
Red Lion PH, Llanbedr
Shops in Crickhowell, 3 miles south Llanbedr

Something that often comes to mind in this part of the world is that there's only one thing worse than a hill so steep you can't ride up it: a hill so steep you can't ride down it. The direction of several of the routes in the Black Mountains is dictated by this principle: better to have a short steep push followed by a long descent than a long climb followed by a descent too steep to ride down. Obviously this is subject to interpretation of what is too steep and the second half of the ride is the exception that proves the rule: the tough 1000 ft descent from the top of Grwyne Fechan down Rhiw Trumau is one of the most testing in the book. The starting point, the Castle Inn at Pengenffordd sells fine beers, has bed and breakfast or bunkhouse accommodation and could be the base for several rides. Ride 13 (Bwlch) and Ride 14 (Mynydd Troed) also start from here. Soon after the start the views open up to the northwest looking across the luscious green pastures of the upper Wye valley. Ahead and to the right lies the escarpment of the Black Mountains. The steep and stony climb to the pass soon follows. After a brief, flat moorland section the superb descent begins, down past the Grwyne Fawr Reservoir following the river valley. A second short climb through forestry leads to another offroad section with fine views east across the Vale of Ewyas. The pub at Llanbedr is the next beacon, reached after a short but lovely section along the lower reaches of the Grwyne Fechan. It is the valley formed by this river that is followed northwards for 7 miles on a remarkably good quality track up to the second major pass. The bone-rattling descent mentioned above is your reward and the Castle Inn beckons.

WARNING This is a tough ride with some exposed sections and should not undertaken in poor weather or in winter except by highly experienced, properly equipped riders.

1 With your back to the Castle Inn, Pengenffordd (on the A479, 3 miles south of Talgarth), **turn R towards Talgarth then 30 yards after the end of the car park**

bear R onto a track running parallel with the road between hedgerows. After 300 yards **turn first R** onto tarmac lane 'No through road.'

2 At fork of tracks **bear R** 'Public Footpath' (it is a RUPP so you can ride it). The track becomes a steep stony push (a mere bagatelle compared to what follows!) Superb, contouring track, likely to be muddy in winter and after prolonged rain. Hills loom ahead.

3 The track joins a tarmac lane by a gate and continues in the same direction. **Easily missed**, cross a cattle grid, then after 1 mile, shortly after passing a house on the left called 'Ffosrhys', **leave the road on a sharp left-hand bend and bear R** onto a track alongside a fence. Follow the track as it swings right uphill.

4 **The Big Climb!** Grassy then very steep stony track. Climb 1150 ft (340 mts) in a mile. This will be a push/carry, probably taking 30 minutes. The views opening up behind are always a good excuse to stop.

5 The track over the top of the moorland is obvious although it will be muddy in winter and after prolonged rain. The track improves as the reservoir comes into sight and you can soon savour a superb descent on good stone surface, with views of the track snaking its way down the valley.

6 Join the tarmac lane and continue down the valley for 3 miles. **Easily missed. Ignore the first two right turns into the forestry** (the second turn is by a small, black, corrugated iron shed). **Turn R uphill on the third forestry road**, opposite a concrete bridge over the river to the left.

7 Climb up through the forestry. At X-roads of tracks bear L 'Bridleway'. After 1/2 mile, **ignore** a bridleway descending to the left. Continue ahead, go through farm/cottage buildings and **turn L** onto broad grassy track.

8 Fine views to the left. Join a tarmac lane and **bear R**. Steep descent, steep climb.

At fork of lanes (GR 278212) **bear R then turn R** *again at T-junction at the bottom of steep hill. The Sugar Loaf looms ahead.*

9 *After ³/4 mile, and almost immediately after passing a road to the left signposted 'Abergavenny 5³/4',* **turn R** *onto track by wall.*

10 *Follow this for 2 miles, crossing a stream and passing farm buildings. At X-roads with tarmac lane go* **SA** *onto track. Descend to the river and take the* **2nd bridge to the L**. *Steep climb. The track turns to tarmac in Llanbedr.* **Bear R then turn R** *to go past the Red Lion PH.*

11 *At T-junction of lanes (GR 236212)* **turn R**. *After 2¹/2 miles, or more relevantly, ¹/2 mile after passing a telephone box, stay on the upper, left-hand lane signposted 'No through road'. Follow the tarmac lane to its end, continuing in the direction of 'Tal y Maes'.*

12 *Pass through a bridlegate next to locked gate, cross bridge and* **fork L**. *Climb steeply. At the next fork* **bear L** *onto earth and stone track alongside wall.*

13 *Superb views ahead. Follow this track for 3 miles, dropping to cross the river via a very handsome stone bridge. Strangely, the path improves as it rises higher. After a final switchback you reach the second major pass of the day, with more fantastic views opening up.*

14 *At the cairn at the pass* **bear R** *downhill (***not** *sharp left on the broader, more obvious track). This becomes a fine, at times technical descent.*

15 *At the road* **turn R then shortly bear L** *at fork of lanes. Descend then climb. On next sharp left-hand bend* **bear R** *onto broad track. Follow this up to the road then* **turn L** *down the road for 50 yards to return to the Castle Inn, Pengenffordd.*

16

DESCENT FROM HEAVEN—
CRUG MAWR FROM CRICKHOWELL

DISTANCE
14 miles (22 kms)

TIME
3 hours

GRADE
Strenuous

TERRAIN
Steep lanes, good stone-based tracks, forestry and superb open grassy descent

HILLS AND HIGHPOINTS
1st climb ▲ 165 ft (50 mts)
out of Crickhowell
2nd climb ▲ 390 ft (120 mts)
up from Llangenny
3rd climb ▲ 505 ft (155 mts)
crossing the Grwyne Fawr to Partrishow
4th climb ▲ 830 ft (255 mts)
from Partrishow Church to Crug Mawr
5th climb ▲ 195 ft (60 mts)
from the river beneath Llanbedr to the
Crickhowell road
Highest point ▲ 1740 feet (530 mts)
Total ascent ▲ 2300 ft (700 mts)

START
The main pay and display car park in Crickhowell, on the A40, 6 miles to the northwest of Abergavenny

PARKING
The pay and display car park in Crickhowell

NEAREST RAILWAY
Abergavenny. Best to head north to Forest Coal Pit and join the route at Partrishow

REFRESHMENTS
Lots of choice in Crickhowell
Dragon's Head Inn, Llangenny
Red Lion PH, Llanbedr

A short but superb ride at the southern end of the Black Mountains with several very steep sections both on road and offroad and one of the finest descents in the whole book on a magnificent grassy track with jaw-dropping views down into the valley formed by Grwyne Fechan.

The ride starts in Crickhowell, one of several fine bases along the Usk Valley. The first testing ascent climbs up from the Red Dragon Inn in Llangenny. This is nothing compared to the next challenge up past Partrishow Church, surely one of the steepest sections of road in the region! A delightful open track contours around the hillside and climbs up alongside then through forestry to emerge on top of Crug Mawr. This marks the start of the dream descent – the track has to be ridden to be believed! The views are stupendous so it is well worthwhile leaving the ride for a clear day. The last offroad section alongside the Grwyne Fechan is also a delight.
So what's left? A few beers in the Red Lion in Llanbedr and the long descent back to Crickhowell.

For a longer ride you could either link to the Llanthony Ride (Ride 17) starting in Stanton or to the Mynydd Du Forestry Ride (Ride 18) starting at the car park at GR 266251.

1 *Exit the car park, return to the A40,* **turn L** *towards Abergavenny then take the* **second road to the L** *at the edge of tow onto Llangenny Lane 'Unsuitable for HGVs'.*

2 *Steady climb, steep descent. At T-junction by the Dragons Head Inn* **turn R to cross bridge, then immediately L** *steeply uphill. At X-roads of lanes by a house called Llanbauffrhwd* **turn L** *uphill onto no through road.*

3 *Further steep climb. Continue* **SA**. **Ignore** *turnings to the right, following signs for Gellirhyd. At the gate with 'Gellirhyd Farm' sign,* **turn L** *downhill onto stone track.* **Ignore** *a track to the left just before a small stone bridge. At the next farm* **turn L** *over the bridge to cross the river, then at T-junction with wider lane* **turn R**.

4 *After 2 miles take the* **1st road to the L** *by a stone barn signposted 'Partrishow Church 1¼' Climb steeply. Shortly, at a T-junction by a newly renovated stone house* **bear L** *uphill.*

5 *Steep descent and exceedingly steep road climb past Partrishow Church. Shortly, after the gradient eases, take the* **1st wide track to the L** *between stone walls.*

6 *Follow this open grassy track to the edge of the forest. At a three way bridleway post* **turn L** *and push your bike steeply uphill alongside the forest. At the X-roads with a wide forest road* **go SA**, *continuing steeply uphill on stony track.*

7 *At T-junction with the next forestry road* **turn L**. *Exit the forest via bridlegate and* **turn R** *uphill alongside fence on grassy track. Go past a gravestone marked with 'Dinas'. After 100 yards join better track and* **turn L**. *You* **are not** *aiming for the trig point on the summit, but following a track parallel to and below the ridge.*

8 *Follow this glorious grassy track for 3 miles, going round a right hand then left hand bend to keep the wall and fence on your left. One steep grassy section (slippery after rain) and one steep, stony, technical section in the woodland.*

9 *At T-junction with farm ahead* **turn L** *downhill on tarmac. At the next farm house* **turn L** *then immediately after the next barn on your left, on a left hand bend in the road,* **turn R** *onto track.*

10 *Lovely riverside section. Take the* **2nd bridge to the L** *over the river and climb steep stony track. At T-junction by the church* **bear R** *(in effect SA).* **Ignore** *a right turn by the Red Lion PH. At the next T-junction* **turn L** *'Crickhowell 2'.*

11 *Follow this road for 2 miles. At T-junction at the end of Great Oak Road* **turn R** *onto Standard Street and follow this as it becomes Greenhill Way to return to the car park.*

17

TWO VALLEYS AND LLANTHONY PRIORY IN THE HEART OF THE BLACK MOUNTAINS

DISTANCE
18 miles (29 kms)

TIME
4 hours

GRADE
Strenuous

TERRAIN
Lanes, farmland, forestry, moorland,
superb valley views

HILLS AND HIGHPOINTS
1st climb ▲ 680 ft (205 mts)
from the start to the highpoint in the forestry
2nd climb ▲ 770 ft (235 mts)
from The Grange Pony Trekking Centre
to the cairn on the ridge. Very steep
3rd climb ▲ 360 ft (110 mts)
from Coed-dias in the Grwyne Fawr
valley to the ridge
Highest point ▲ 2035 ft (620 mts)
at the cairn on the ridge between the valleys
Total ascent ▲ 2570 ft (785 mts)

START
The Queens Head PH car park at Stanton,
6 miles to the north of Abergavenny on the
road to Llanthony (GR 311222)

PARKING
The Queens Head PH car park
Please pay £1 to the inn, please do not abuse
the system

NEAREST RAILWAY
Abergavenny, 6 miles to the south

REFRESHMENTS
Queens Head PH, Stanton
Travellers Rest PH at Llanthony Priory
Half Moon Hotel, Llanthony

A superb ride linking two beautiful valleys in the heart of the Black Mountains with one very steep, rough climb between the two which will involve some carrying. It is certainly worth poking your nose around Llanthony Priory, a beautiful ruin in an idyllic setting with the chance of a coffee or a beer to fortify you for the big climb later in the ride.

The ride starts from the car park of the Queens Head in Stanton–please pay them £1 before setting off. A very steep climb on tarmac marks the start of the ride and if you are feeling a bit bleary you could be excused for walking this part before you are warmed up. The undulating forestry track offers magnificent views down into the Vale of Ewyas and across to the cliffs on the edge of Hatterrall Hill. Beyond Llanthony there is a choice – follow the valley road, which can get busy at the weekends and in summer, or take the parallel lanes and tracks (some of them rough) and avoid the possibility of traffic. Beyond the Grange Trekking Centre in Capel-y-ffin you are faced with a very steep, rough, strenuous climb up the side of the escarpment. This will probably take about 30 minutes and the views behind are a good excuse to stop. From the large cairn at the top there is a short section on sheep tracks before joining the glorious descent on forestry roads then lanes to Coed-dias. A final push takes you back onto the ridge for some of the best views of the day, looking down into both valleys. You will need good brakes on the hill back to the start!

WARNING! The climb up from Capel-y-ffin should only be undertaken by strong and fit cyclists in conditions of good visibility. It is worth considering padding on the frame to help you can carry your bike comfortably.

1 With back to the Queens Head PH in Stanton **turn R then L** steeply uphill on tarmac lane. Very steep climb. After ¹⁄₂ mile take the 1st broad, forestry track to the right towards green barrier.

2 Gradient eases. Follow undulating forest track for 5 miles with superb valley views to the right. At T-junction on steeper descent (GR 293267) **turn sharp R** downhill. At T-junction with the road **turn L**.

3 Cross river, go through Llanthony, passing the priory on your right. At fork of lanes immediately after the Half Moon Hotel **bear R** onto no through road. At the end of the tarmac, with gates all around, go **SA**

through wooden gate onto broad enclosed track.

4 At junction with road go **SA**. **(In winter/after prolonged rain**, to avoid 200 yds quagmire section at GR 259311, **turn L** at junction with road, cross the river then **turn R**. Follow this lane for 2¹⁄₂ miles and take the first lane/'No through road' **to the L** 'Grange Trekking Centre')*.

5 Main/summer route. Go past several farms and through several gates, continuing in the same direction. Tarmac turns to track. Dog leg left then right past a final farm onto a steep and stony track. Muddy section. Cross river via wooden bridge then climb short, steep, stony track to the road **turn R**.

6 After ¹⁄₂ mile take the **1st L** steeply uphill on no through road 'Grange Trekking Centre' then shortly **1st L** again on tarmac drive 'Public Bridleway' and follow this steeply uphill past buildings as it turns to track and leads onto the moorland via gate at the top of stone and railway sleeper track. Stay close to the forest and climb very steeply.

7 Near the end of the forest **bear R** to follow stream valley then cross stream at obvious point and follow the green grassy track that zig zags up the escarpment ahead. Hard push on rough stony track. Some carrying sections. Follow the obvious track to the large stone cairn on the ridge.

8 Cross the main ridge path and go **SA** onto less defined path. Shortly **bear L** and contour towards the start of the forestry track almost due south of the cairn (there are no waymarks and no main track – use the sheep tracks where possible). The bridlegate into the forest is 150 yards downhill from the stile at the start of the forestry road.

9 Follow the narrow stony track downhill round sharp right hand then left hand hairpin bends. At junction with forestry track continue **SA downhill*** and enjoy the glorious 3 mile descent. At the road **turn L**.

* (If you wish to extend the ride and do a tour of Mynydd Du Forest you can link

with **Ride 18** by taking the **1st track to the R** after 200 yds by a 3 way 'Bridleway' sign. Join the other ride at Instruction 2 GR 250289**)**.

10 **Main route** *After 2½ miles on road, opposite a telephone box standing between two tall ash trees* **turn L** *over the bridge (this is the second bridge to the left). Climb past farm, pass between stone wall and metal fence onto narrow stony track.*

11 *Final climb of the day. At the top* **bear R** *alongside the wall. Fine views of both valleys. At fork of tracks after ¾ mile* **bear L** *(GR 287233). Follow this glorious track as it turns to tarmac and descends steeply back to the start.*

18

A CIRCUIT OF MYNYDD DU FOREST, NORTH OF ABERGAVENNY

DISTANCE
11 miles (18 kms)

TIME
2 hours

GRADE
Moderate

TERRAIN
Forestry with some fine valley views. Mainly forest roads with some narrower, steeper bridleway sections

HILLS AND HIGHPOINTS
1st (steep) climb ▲ 525 ft (160 mts) at the start
2nd (steady) climb ▲ 260 ft (80 mts)
3rd (steady climb) ▲ 655 ft (200 mts)
Highest point ▲ 1905 feet (580 mts)
Total ascent ▲ 1800 ft (550 mts)

START
The car park at GR 266251 on the minor road leading towards Grwyne Fawr Reservoir. This is best approached from the A465 north of Abergavenny (leave at Llanvihangel Crucorney) then aim for Stanton and follow signs for Grwyne Fawr and Mynydd Du Forestry Commission. The car park is the first on the right (Ffawyddog)

PARKING
The car park at GR 266251

NEAREST RAILWAY
Abergavenny

REFRESHMENTS
None on the route, nearest is the Queens Head PH at Stanton

There are six major forestry holdings in the area covered by this book. For details of the other five see 'Other routes in brief/Forestry' at the front of the book.
Of all of them, Mynydd Du Forest perhaps offers the greatest scope for designing your own tailor-made route complete with single track options.

DIRECTIONS   *A circuit of Mynydd Du Forest, north of Abergavenny*

My apologies in advance for those of you who expect this forest ride to be full of single track! Imagine the difficulty in describing any route in the forest, even those using the main forest roads without the guidewriter's usual props of signposts, pubs, farms or churches to act as bearings and with a vocabulary limited to left, right, up or down. Now compound this by throwing in some single track. See what I mean? Use this ride as a coathanger on which to hang your own routes. Or link it to Rides 16 or 17 for a longer challenge. Sufficient height is gained for there to be excellent views in all of the clearings and having said what I did about single track, there is a fairly testing bridleway near the end of the route.

1 *From the Ffawddydog Forestry Commission car park at GR 267251, go back towards the road but **bear R before the bridge**. Climb steeply alongside stream/ waterfall and mixed woodland. At T-junction at the top **bear L**.*

2 *Fast descent. At T-junction (GR 249269) **bear R** uphill. Steady climb. **Easy to miss**, after 2 miles, and 100 yards **before a sharp right hand hairpin bend, bear L** downhill on narrower track marked by 'Blaen y cwm. Bridleway' wooden signpost (GR 250289).*

3 *At T-junction with broad stone track **turn L**. At T-junction with tarmac lane **turn R** then after 300 yards **turn L** downhill to cross the bridge over the river. At the end of the bridge go **SA** steeply uphill for 50 yards and **turn R** onto broad stone and grassy forest track. Climb steadily.*

4 *At T-junction with more defined forestry track **bear R** uphill (GR 242289) then shortly at next T-junction **turn L** gently downhill (GR 243287).*

5 *Follow this broad forest road for 2 miles, going round two wide sweeping bends around gullies/streams descending the hillside. At the next junction **bear R** uphill (GR 250268) then after ½ mile, at the next T-junction **turn L** downhill (GR 246263).*

6 *Long descent over 3 miles. **Easy to miss**, soon after the start of a climb after this long descent, and with the end of the forest a few hundred yards ahead **turn L** by a bridleway sign onto steep, narrow, stony track.*

7 *Shortly, at X-roads with next forest road continue **SA** on second, shorter, steep stony narrow track. At T-junction with broader track **turn L** towards the farm.*

8 *Follow the track round to the right between farm buildings. Take either track at the fork–they link up. At X-roads of forest tracks **turn R** downhill, then cross the road to return to the car park at the start.*

19

LORD HEREFORD'S KNOB FROM VELINDRE, SOUTH OF HAY-ON-WYE

DISTANCE
16 miles (26 kms)

TIME
4 hours

GRADE
Strenuous

TERRAIN
Wooded slopes, steep grassy climb up the escarpment. Tracks through sheep pastures, hedgerows and stonewalls

HILLS AND HIGHPOINTS
It is a climb almost from the start right up to Lord Hereford's Knob ▲ 720 ft (220 mts) on tarmac, 820 ft (250 mts) offroad with one exceedingly steep grassy section straight up the hillside
Highest point ▲ 2035 feet (620 mts) just below Lord Hereford's Knob
Total ascent ▲ 2070 ft (630 mts)

START
Velindre, a small village on the minor road between Talgarth and Hay-on-Wye (3 miles northeast of Talgarth)

PARKING
Parking near the playground in Velindre (towards Talgarth from the pub)

NEAREST RAILWAY
Abergavenny, 14 miles from the route at Capel y Ffin

REFRESHMENTS
Three Horseshoes PH, Felindre
The pub at Llanthony is 4 miles off the route down the Vale of Ewyas

The offroad climb (push/struggle/haul!) up the hillside towards Lord Hereford's Knob (jokes on a postcard, please) is one of the steepest in the book. However, as compensation the views back down into the Wye Valley are fabulous and the long descent down into the Vale of Ewyas improves almost with each turn of the pedal.

Felindre, or Velindre as it is marked on the map, is chosen as the starting point because of its fine pub and conveniently located car park. Although an obvious bridleway leads southeast from the village alongside Felindre Brook, do not be tempted! Imagine the worst damage that hundreds of horses could do to a track, double it and there you have the state of the bridleway right up to its junction with the lane below the escarpment.

So the quiet dead-end road leading past Pen yr Heol chapel is chosen as a less stressful alternative. The track contouring around the end of Darren Lwyd is better on its western side, but the views are so wonderful that it is hardly a problem to walk sections of the bridleway on its course northwards to the Gospel Pass road. The lane descent from the top of Gospel Pass is the stuff of dreams: fast, open with magnificent views ahead. The temptation to let rip and end up in Hay-on-Wye may be too great to resist. The route described below drops down into the valley formed by the Digedi Brook: the track crosses the stream three times and each crossing offers the options of a footbridge or a ford. Wildflowers and stone walls line the final section of the track before it turns to tarmac. The last few miles are on road but the lane is fairly quiet and there's always the pub in Felindre to look forward to!

1 *From the Three Horseshoes PH, Velindre (GR 186366) follow the main road northeast towards Hay-on-Wye. After 1 mile,* **take the second R** *signposted 'Pen Yr Heol Chapel 1'.*

2 *At the end of the tarmac go* **SA** *through two gates onto an enclosed track. At the gate at the end of the enclosed section continue* **SA** *aiming towards the green track that goes straight up the steep hillside. This swings sharp right some way above the final trees.*

3 *At the top go* **SA** *on obvious track and follow for 2 miles. Most of this is rideable, although there will be sections where you need to dismount. The valley gradually becomes wooded.*

4 *The track broadens then turns to tarmac. 300 yards after the gate by farm and barn keep an eye out for blue arrow on a wooden marker post and* **bear L** *onto a track parallel with the road.*

5 *The track contours southeast around the end of Darren Lwyd and heads back NNW above and parallel to the road in the valley below. The second half of this contouring track is rougher with longer sections that cannot be cycled.*

6 *Join the road,* **bear L**, *climb to the top of Gospel Pass and descend gloriously for 1½ miles before taking the first road to the left 'National Cycle Network Route 42'.*

7 *After a further mile,* **take the second track to the R**, *by a triangle of grass 'Bridleway. Llanigon 4.5 kms'. As the broad gravel track swings right* **bear L** *(in effect SA) through gate 'Bridleway'. (The bridleway is the sunken track. It does improve!).*

8 *The track crosses the stream then after ½ mile crosses it twice more in quick succession. The track widens and improves, although beware of the drainage channels that run across the track at right angles. The track turns to tarmac for a fast descent.*

9 *At T-junction of lanes* **turn L then shortly 1st R.**

10 *At T-junction near to telephone box* **bear L** *and follow this road for 3 miles back to the Three Horseshoes PH in Felindre.*

20

OLCHON VALLEY, BLACK HILL AND CRASWALL, SOUTH OF HAY-ON-WYE

DISTANCE
12 miles (19 kms)

TIME
3 hours

GRADE
Strenuous

TERRAIN
Faint track over moorland, wooded valley, sheep pasture, hedgerows and woodland

HILLS AND HIGHPOINTS
1st climb (push) ▲ 700 ft (215 mts)
with difficult route-finding in poor visibility
2nd climb (on road) ▲ 165 ft (50 mts)
at the southern end of Black Hill
3rd climb ▲ 560 ft (170 mts)
from Craswall back towards the start
Highest point ▲ 2165 feet (660 mts)
Total ascent ▲ 1700 ft (520 mts)

START
The car park at GR 240373 on the Gospel Pass road between Hay-on-Wye and Abergavenny.
From Hay-on-Wye: Follow the B4350 towards Talgarth. Go past The Swan Hotel then take the next left on Forest Road signposted 'Capel y Ffin'. After 3 miles fork right by a triangle of grass ('Craswall' is signposted to the left) The car park is 2 miles along this road, after passing the first lane to the right

PARKING
The car park at GR 240373

NEAREST RAILWAY
Abergavenny, 15 miles south of Black Hill

REFRESHMENTS
A good pub, the Bulls Head Inn at Craswall

A ride with two very different halves: the first half is pure moorland, with potential difficulty in route-finding, a steep climb up onto the ridge of Hay Bluff with magnficent views on a clear day. The second half is lower, flatter and much more rooted in a landscape gently altered by man and sheep as the path crosses long stretches of pasture, passing through many gates along the track.

The linking section between the two halves offers the finest views and the best descent as you drop down from the high moorland into the wooded and half-forgotten Olchon Valley. With a starting point at almost 1500 ft, this is definitely a ride to be undertaken only in fine weather, partly because the views will be non-existent in mist and partly because the outward track is sufficiently faint for it to cause route-finding problems even in good visibility. Once you have found the top of the valley of Olchon Brook the views are film set material. The descent is rocky for short sections and will probably require you to dismount at times. Savour those views and give your aching muscles a rest! There is a strange, deserted air about the upper road section of the valley with several ruins of bygone farms. Before long a sign for a picnic site brings you back to this century. The second half of the ride is much more pastoral with some muddy sections of track and many field edges to cross. You will probably cover this stretch at 2-3 mph! Enjoy the views down into the valley of the River Monnow, which passes through Monmouth and joins the Wye on its way to Chepstow. The outward route is finally rejoined and before long you are back at the Gospel Pass road.

WARNING! *Not to be attempted in poor visibility. This is a slow ride and may easily take 3 hours to complete.*

1 *From the car park on the Gospel Pass Hay–Llanthony road, at GR 240373 head downhill on the road for 200 yards back towards Hay.* **Easy to miss. 50 yards before the round green plastic grit bin, turn R** *by a stone marked with a yellow arrow onto a grassy/earth track.*

2 *After 300 yards at fork of tracks just after crossing a small stream* **bear R.** *At a second stream crossing leave the main, rutted track and* **bear R** *onto a grassy track that visibly climbs southeast across the face of the hillside up towards the ridge extending back from Hay Bluff.*

3 *This track is at times faint. If in doubt keep climbing, the track heads due south at one point before emerging on the ridge path near to a distinctive 'lump' at GR 255355.* **Do not climb up onto this lump but bear L** *before it onto a track that contours beneath it.*

4 *Emerge at a cairn/shrine. Leave this to your right, continue in the same direction, below the ridge.* **Easily missed,** *the ridge is finally crossed at the lowest point of a gentle dip and you soon find yourself in the valley formed by Olchon Brook. The views are spectacular, the track is largely rideable (there are some rocky sections where you may prefer to dismount).*

5 *Join the road and* **bear L.** *This is an amazing 'forgotten' valley with lots of ruins of old farmhouses. After 1¼ miles take the* **1st tarmac lane to the L** *'Picnic Site'. At the end of the steep lane continue* **SA** *through gate onto track 'Bridleway'.*

6 *Fine track with good views to the right. Sections may be muddy in winter or after prolonged rain. Briefly join tarmac lane. At a triangle of grass where the lane swings right downhill* **bear L** *onto the track signposted 'Bridleway'. (If you wish to go to the pub at Craswall, follow the road downhill,* **turn L** *at the X-roads and continue up the valley for 1½ miles).*

7 *Over the next 2 miles the bridleway passes through innumerable gates and along field edges. Sections of this will get very muddy in winter and it is worth following the pub route and the lane past College Farm to its end as a winter/wet weather alternative.*

8 *The scenery opens up after a stream crossing. There are many tracks heading in the same direction but as long as you continue generally parallel to the Hay Bluff ridge to your left and avoid dropping into the valleys off to your right you will end up rejoining the outward route and return to the road.* **Turn left** *uphill for the car park.*